MEDITERRANEAN

a taste of the sun in over 150 recipes

MEDITERRANEAN

a taste of the sun in over 150 recipes

JACQUELINE CLARK and **JOANNA FARROW**

H
HERMES
HOUSE

This edition published by Hermes House in 2003

© Anness Publishing Limited 1996, 2003

Hermes House is an imprint of
Anness Publishing Limited
Hermes House
88–89 Blackfriars Road
London SE1 8HA

A CIP catalogue record for this book is available from the British Library.

Publisher: Joanna Lorenz
Senior Cookery Editor: Linda Fraser
Designer: Nigel Partridge
Photography and styling: Michelle Garrett, assisted by Dulce Riberio
Food for photography: Jacqueline Clark and Joanna Farrow
Illustrator: Anna Koska

Front cover shows Black Pasta with Squid Sauce. For recipe see page 114.
Previously published as *Taste of the Mediterranean*

5 7 9 10 8 6 4

NOTES
For all recipes, quantities are given in both metric and imperial measures and, where
appropriate, measures are also given in standard cups and spoons.
Follow one set, but not a mixture, because they are not interchangeable.
Standard spoon and cup measures are level.
1 tsp = 5ml, 1 tbsp = 15ml, 1 cup = 250ml/8fl oz
Australian standard tablespoons are 20ml. Australian readers should use 3 tsp in place of 1 tbsp for
measuring small quantities of gelatine, cornflour, salt, etc.
Medium eggs are used unless otherwise stated.

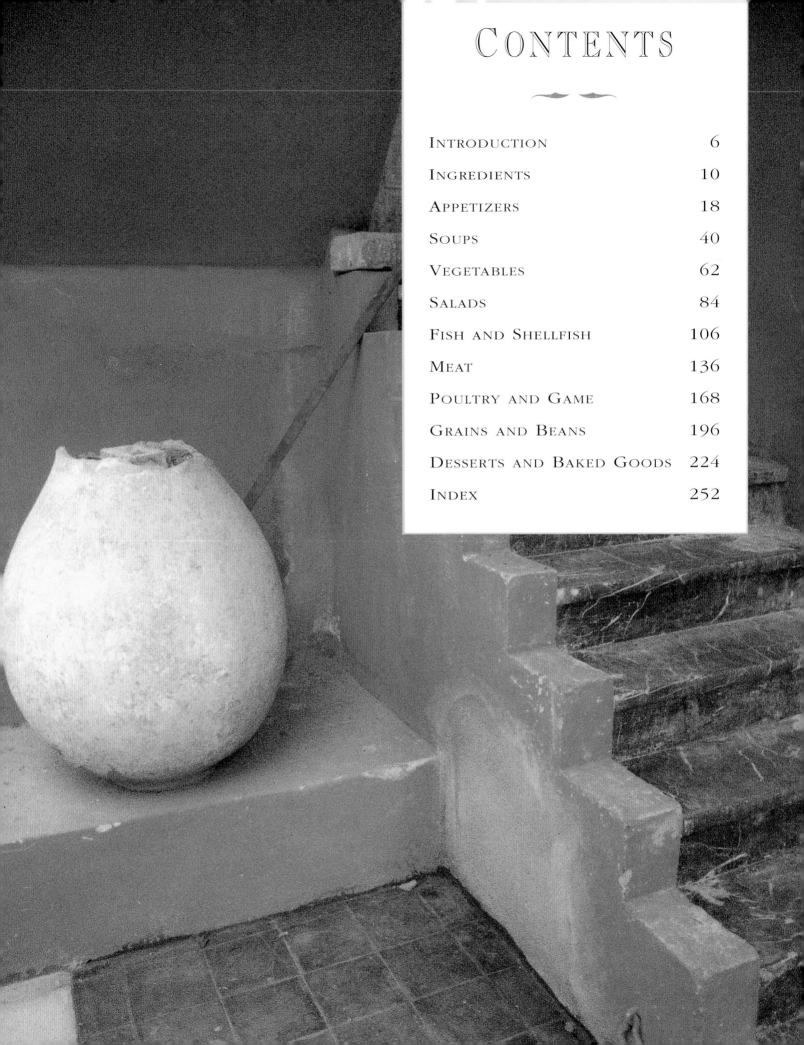

CONTENTS

INTRODUCTION

The countries bordered by the Mediterranean sea
produce some of the finest food the world has to
offer—set sail with us on a culinary tour.

ABOVE: A grove of old olive trees lit by the afternoon sun in Provence.

Azure skies, even bluer seas, white-gold sands, bright, whitewashed walls, the vibrant reds, greens, yellows, purples and oranges of the flowers, fruits and vegetables on display in the market—these are the paint palette colors of the Mediterranean. These evocative images are familiar to many of us, although, of course, we will not all be thinking of the same country—after all, there are fifteen to consider. A quick tour will take us from the shores of Spain, to France, Italy, Greece, Turkey, Syria, Lebanon, Israel, and into Africa to Egypt, Libya, Tunisia, Algeria and Morocco. The islands of Malta and Cyprus are truly Mediterranean, encircled by the sea. In many ways these fifteen countries are completely different from each other, but one thread links them all—the love of good food.

Centuries before Christ, the area surrounding the Mediterranean sea was colonized by the Phoenicians, Greeks and Romans, who shared a basic cultivation of wheat, olives and grapes. These, in turn, became bread, oil and wine, three components that are still very important in today's Mediterranean diet. With the building of ships came import and export, and the various countries began a sort of cross-pollination of crops, ingredients and recipes. Spices and flavorings were introduced through North Africa and Arabia, and saffron, cloves, chiles, ginger and allspice continue to be popular all over the Mediterranean, appearing in sweet and savory dishes. Nuts, too, are an ingredient common to many of the countries. Almonds, pistachios and pine nuts are perhaps the most popular, as they are native to the region.

When thinking of Mediterranean food, however, it is the fresh fruit, vegetables and herbs that immediately spring to mind. Open-air markets from Marseilles to Morocco are a feast for the senses. Fabulous arrays of

tomatoes, eggplant, zucchini, peaches, figs, garlic and pungent herbs such as basil and thyme are tantalizingly displayed; the experience is completed by the hot sun drawing out the flavors and aromas. Mediterranean cooking depends on the freshest of ingredients; it is honest, simple and prepared with respect.

Recent research has proved the Mediterranean diet to be a very healthy one, thus increasing its popularity. Olive oil is at the heart of this theory; it contains a high proportion of monounsaturated fats. Olive oils vary in color, from the golden Spanish varieties to the deep greens of some Greek, Provençal and Italian oils. Color is not really an indication of quality; the oils have to be tasted, and flavor, like color, varies immensely.

BELOW: Glossy green leaves shade juicy oranges in a grove near Seville.

ABOVE: Melons, including the familiar tiger watermelons in the background, lie piled in the sun in a Greek market.

The people of the Mediterranean have known great hardship and poverty. Although we may have images of endless sunny days, the weather can be wild and unjust. Lack of rain, terrible winds and a capricious sea ruin crops and the fishermen's haul; in the past, foreign domination and disease caused poverty and death. Because of this, the most basic foods are, even today, a celebration of life to the Mediterranean people. Bread is an important staple and always accompanies a meal, be it a bowl of soup or a platter of grilled fish.

Perhaps Mediterranean food could be described as "peasant food," not in a derogatory sense, but as an homage to the people who have provided and inspired us with such a vast and wonderful repertoire of recipes, ancient and new. In this book, we give you just a few of the countless dishes from around the Mediterranean. Some are traditional—for example, Gazpacho, Ratatouille, Greek Salad and Provençal Beef Daube, while others are more contemporary, using Mediterranean ingredients but creating something new. Among these recipes are Grilled Vegetable Terrine, Pan-fried Red Mullet with Basil, Mushroom and Pesto Pizza, and Turkish Delight Ice Cream.

As in the Mediterranean, ingredients should be fresh and of the highest quality, even if this means waiting for some of them, such as tomatoes or figs, to be in season. We hope to bring you a true taste of the Mediterranean.

INGREDIENTS

VEGETABLES

ARTICHOKES There are two types of artichoke, in no way related: the globe, which belongs to the thistle family, and the Jerusalem, which is a tuber, belonging to the sunflower family. The globe artichoke is common throughout the Mediterranean, appearing as different varieties, depending on the country. When buying, choose firm, taut specimens. After boiling, the ends of the leaves and base are edible. Baby varieties are completely edible and are sometimes eaten raw. Jerusalem artichokes look like knobbly potatoes, and can be treated as such.

EGGPLANT Although eggplant originated in Asia, it is featured in dishes from every Mediterranean country. There are many different varieties, including green, white and yellow, but the plump purple variety is the most common. Look for firm, taut, shiny-skinned specimens with green stalks. Eggplant is sometimes salted and drained before cooking, which helps to extract bitter juices and makes it absorb less oil during cooking.

FAVA OR BROAD BEANS Fava beans were the only beans known in Europe before the discovery of the New World. When young, fava beans can be cooked and eaten, pods and

Fennel

all, or shelled and eaten raw with cheese, as in Italy. When the beans are older, they are shelled, cooked, and sometimes peeled. Dried fava beans are popular in the Middle East, where they are cooked with spices or added to stews.

FENNEL This white bulb of overlapping leaves and green, feathery fronds has a fresh anise flavor and can be eaten cooked or raw. Its flavor complements fish and chicken, but it is also delicious served as a separate vegetable course, either roasted or baked with a cheese sauce. Choose firm, rounded bulbs, and use the fronds for garnishing. If using raw, toss the slices in lemon juice to prevent them from discoloring.

MUSHROOMS The varieties used in Mediterranean cooking are button, open-cup and flat, but regional wild species, such as cèpes, chanterelles and oyster mushrooms, can be found in the markets during autumn.

OKRA This African vegetable, sometimes called lady fingers, is a long five-sided green pod, with a tapering end. It has a subtle flavor and a gelatinous texture that helps to thicken and enrich certain dishes. Used in Middle Eastern and Greek cooking, its most successful partners are garlic, onion and tomatoes. Choose small, firm specimens and use sliced or whole in cooking.

Artichokes

Okra

ONIONS The starting point of so many dishes, the onion is invaluable to Mediterranean cooking. There are many varieties, differing in color, size and strength of flavor. For salads, or when onion is to be used raw, choose red or white-skinned varieties that have a sweet, mild flavor. The large Spanish onions have a mild flavor too, and are a good choice when a large quantity of onion is called for in a recipe. Pearl onions are perfect for adding whole to stews, or serving as a vegetable dish on their own.

PEPPERS Sweet bell peppers add color to markets across the Mediterranean region. To make the most of their flavor, broil peppers until the skins are charred, then rub off and discard the skins. Marinate the peppers in olive oil.

RADICCHIO This red chicory is very popular in Italy. There are several varieties, but the most common is the round variety that looks like a little lettuce. The leaves are crisp and pleasantly bitter and can be eaten raw or cooked. Radicchio is delicious broiled and drizzled with olive oil and sprinkled with black pepper, or shredded and stirred into risotto or spaghetti. The raw leaves make a colorful addition to salads.

RADISHES These are best eaten raw to appreciate their peppery flavor—serve them as the French do, with salt and butter, or use them as a colorful addition to a platter of crudites.

SPINACH This leaf vegetable is very popular in the Mediterranean countries. Cooked or raw, it is a good source of vitamins A and C. Young spinach leaves can be eaten raw and need little preparation, but older leaves should be washed in several changes of water and then picked over and the tough stalks removed. Spinach is used in Middle Eastern pastries, Spanish tapas, French tarts and many more dishes—eggs and fish, for example, make good partners. A little doesn't go a long way—if the spinach is to be cooked, allow 8 ounces raw weight per person.

TOMATOES Some of the best tomatoes are to be found in Mediterranean markets. Sun-ripened and full of flavor, they come in many varieties—beefsteak tomatoes for slicing, plum tomatoes, vine tomatoes, cherry tomatoes and baby pear-shaped ones. Cooked with onion and garlic, tomatoes make the universal sauce that so many Mediterranean dishes rely on. Canned and sun-dried tomatoes are invaluable items to keep in the pantry.

Radishes

Vine tomatoes

GRAPE LEAVES These pretty leaves have been used in cooking for hundreds of years. They can be stuffed with a variety of fillings and also make perfect wrappers for meat, fish and poultry. Fresh leaves must be young and soft. If using brined grape leaves, soak them in hot water for 20–30 minutes before stuffing or wrapping.

ZUCCHINI These green squashes are at their best when they are small. They can be eaten raw and have a good flavor and crisp texture. The larger they become, the less flavor they have. When buying, choose firm, shiny specimens. Yellow varieties are sometimes available and, although there is no difference in flavor, they make a pretty alternative to the usual green variety. In Italy and France, the golden flowers are stuffed and cooked, or deep-fried in batter.

OLIVES

The fruit of one of the earliest-known trees native to the Mediterranean. There are hundreds of varieties, differing widely in size, quality and taste. Color depends purely on ripeness—the fruit changes from yellow to green, violet, purple, brown and finally black when fully ripened. Fresh olives are picked at the desired stage of ripeness, then soaked in water, bruised and immersed in brine to produce the familiar-tasting result. They can be bought whole or pitted, sometimes stuffed with bell peppers, anchovies or nuts, or in jars with flavorings such as garlic, coriander, chile and herbs.

DAIRY PRODUCTS

CHEESE The range of cheeses from Mediterranean countries is diverse—varieties are made from cow's, goat's, sheep's and, in the case of Italian mozzarella, water buffalo's milk. Cream cheese is also common to many countries, varying a little according to the milk and the method used for preparing it.

YOGURT This live product (pasteurized milk combined with two beneficial bacteria) is perhaps most associated with the Middle Eastern countries, where it is used extensively in cooking. Greek yogurt is thick and creamy, and French yogurt is traditionally of the set variety. It is used as a marinade, a dip and to enrich soups and stews, and can be made from goat's, sheep's or cow's milk.

GRAINS

BULGUR Also known as cracked wheat, this cereal has been partially processed, and so cooks quickly. It can be used in place of rice as an accompaniment to broiled meats, as a stuffing, mixed with ground meat to make patties, or in salads, such as tabbouleh.

COUSCOUS This is a product made from semolina. The grains have been rolled, dampened and coated with the fine wheat flour. The commercial variety simply needs moistening, then steaming to swell the grains and produce a soft texture. It is the staple of the North African diet and is usually served with a spicy meat or vegetable stew, but it can also be used as a stuffing or in salads.

RICE There are many varieties of this worldwide staple food. In Italy there are at least four short-grained types used for risotto, and in Spain, Valencia rice is the preferred variety for paella. In the Middle East it is served with every meal, either plainly boiled or cooked with saffron and spices to create fragrant pilafs.

FRUIT

DATES Although fresh dates are quite widely available today, the dried variety remains an invaluable addition to cakes and quick breads. Fresh dates should be plump

Sea Bass

and slightly wrinkled and have a rich, honeylike flavor and dense texture. They are best treated simply, or pitted and served with thick strained yogurt.

FIGS This fruit is associated with all the Mediterranean countries. Different varieties vary in skin color, from dark purple to green to a golden yellow, but all are made up of hundreds of tiny seeds surrounded by soft pink flesh. Choose firm unblemished fruit that just yield to the touch. Treat them simply, or serve with prosciutto or plain yogurt and honey.

MELONS This fruit comes in many different sizes, shapes and colors—cantaloupe, charentais, galia, honeydew, ogen, orange- and green-fleshed varieties, and the wonderful pink watermelon. Ripe melons should yield to gentle pressure at the stem end and have a fragrant scent. Rarely used in cooked dishes, they are best eaten chilled by the slice or as part of a fruit salad.

PEACHES AND NECTARINES Peaches need plenty of sun to ripen them. They grow in France, Spain and Italy. There are yellow-, pink- and white-fleshed varieties; some are clingstone, where the flesh clings to the pit, while others are of the freestone variety. Look for bruise-free specimens that just give when squeezed gently.

Figs

Nectarines are smooth-skinned, with all the luscious flavor of the peach.

ORANGES This fruit is grown all over the Mediterranean, particularly in Spain. Seville oranges, the bitter marmalade variety, have a short season in January. The best of the flavor comes from the zest—the outer layer of the skin— and this is often included in recipes using oranges.

FISH AND SEAFOOD

RED MULLET Very popular along the coasts of the Mediterranean, the red mullet is a pretty fish. It is usually treated simply by grilling over a wood fire. It can also be filleted and pan-fried, or included in delicious fish soups. Snapper makes a good alternative.

SEA BASS This fish is usually sold and cooked whole. The flesh is soft and delicate and needs careful attention when cooking. Cooking methods include poaching, steaming, broiling and baking.

SQUID Very popular in the Mediterranean, particularly in Spain, Italy and Portugal. Squid vary in size from the tiny specimens that can be eaten whole to the larger varieties, which are good for stuffing, broiling or stewing. The flesh is sweet and, when cooked for a short time, tender. Long cooking will also produce succulent results. Sometimes the ink is used to make a sauce for the squid.

SALT COD Most salt cod is prepared in Norway, Iceland and Newfoundland and then exported to Mediterranean countries. It is gutted, cleaned and soaked in brine, then dried. The end result looks very unappetizing, with a

pungent smell, but after soaking for 48 hours and cooking in the Mediterranean style, it is delicious.

TUNA An oily fish belonging to the same family as the mackerel. The flesh, which is sold in steaks or large pieces, is richly flavored, firmly textured, dark red and very dense, and has a tendency to dry out when cooked. Marinating before cooking helps to keep the flesh moist, as does basting while cooking. Tuna can be baked, fried, broiled or stewed.

CRAB There are thousands of species of crab around the world. In the Mediterranean countries, brown and spider crabs are the most common. The meat of the crab is divided into two types—brown and white. Crabs are often sold cooked and dressed, which means that the crab has been prepared and is ready to eat. Choose heavy cooked crabs, which should have a lot of meat.

MUSSELS Available in the Mediterranean from September to April, mussels usually need to be scrubbed and have the beard—the hairy tuft attached to the shell—removed. Any open mussels should be discarded if they do not close after a sharp tap. Mussels vary in size, and the shell can be blue-black to dappled brown. They are easy to cook—just steam for a few minutes in a covered pan.

SHRIMP These vary enormously in size. The classic Mediterranean shrimp is large, about 8 inches, reddish brown in color when raw, and pink when cooked. When shrimp are cooked over strong heat, as on a barbecue, the shell is often left on to protect the flesh from charring.

BEANS

CHICKPEAS These look like pale golden hazelnuts and are sold either dried or already cooked. Chickpeas have a nutty flavor and are used in stews from North Africa to Spain. In the Middle East they are made into flour, and in Greece they are puréed to produce a delicious dip. Soak them for at least 5 hours before cooking. They may have to be cooked for up to 4 hours before they become tender. This varies according to the age of the chickpeas.

LENTILS These come in different sizes and can be yellow, red, brown or green. The tiny green Puy lentils are favored in France and the brown and red ones in the Middle East, where they are cooked with spices to make dhals. They are also used in soups and need no soaking time, cooking in under an hour.

NAVY BEANS These small, plump white beans, which are quite soft when cooked, are used in casseroles in Spain and Portugal, as well as the famous cassoulet in France. They need to be soaked for 3–4 hours before cooking, and are also good in soups and salads.

PASTA

Pasta is simply the Latin word for "paste," the flour-and-egg-based dough from which it is made. Although a staple of Italian cooking, pasta is widely used throughout the Mediterranean and has much in common with Chinese noodles, which filtered from China via the Middle Eastern trade routes. In Italy today there are countless varieties, from flat sheets of lasagne and ribbon noodles to pressed and molded shapes, specifically designed to pocket substantial amounts of the sauce they are served with. Dried pasta makes a good standby, but fresh pasta has a better flavor and texture and freezes well. Both can

Shrimp

Toasted pine nuts

be bought flavored with tomato, olive, spinach or mushroom paste. Black pasta, made with the addition of squid ink, is increasingly popular. Homemade pasta is easy to make if time is allowed for chilling the fresh dough. Rolling it can be done effortlessly using a pasta machine.

NUTS

ALMONDS Cultivated commercially in Spain, Italy and Portugal, the almond is widely used in the Arab-influenced countries. It is an important ingredient in sweet pastries and is often added to savory dishes, too. Almonds are sold fresh in their velvety green shells in the Mediterranean markets.

PINE NUTS These little nuts are used in both sweet and savory dishes, and are one of the principal ingredients in pesto, the basil sauce from Italy.

PISTACHIOS This colorful nut originated in the Middle East. It has flesh that ranges from pale to dark green, and a papery, purple-tinged skin. Pistachio nuts have a subtle flavor and are used in a wide range of dishes, from pastries (both sweet and savory) to ice creams and nougat.

WALNUTS This very versatile nut is used in both sweet and savory dishes. Walnut oil is a popular ingredient in salad dressings in France. Elsewhere, walnuts are chopped and added to pastries, ground to make sauces, or eaten fresh.

HERBS

BASIL One of the herbs most crucial to Mediterranean cooking, particularly in Italian dishes. The sweet tender leaves have a great affinity for tomatoes, eggplant, peppers, zucchini and cheese. A handful of torn leaves livens up a green salad and can be packed into a bottle of olive oil to produce an aromatic flavor.

BAY These hardy leaves are taken from the bay shrub or tree and are widely used to flavor slow-cooked dishes like stocks, soups and stews. They are also added to marinades, threaded onto kebab skewers, thrown on the grill to invigorate the smoky flavor, or used for decorative purposes. One or two young bay leaves, infused with milk or cream in desserts, add a warm, pungent flavor.

BOUQUET GARNI A collection of herbs that traditionally includes parsley, thyme and bay, although other herbs, such as rosemary and marjoram, can be added. Available dried, tied in muslin bundles or in tea bag-like sachets. Fresh bouquet garni can be tied together with string for easy removal from the dish before serving.

CHERVIL This delicate, pretty-leaved, gentle herb is rather like a mild parsley and needs to be used generously to impart sufficient flavor. Widely used in French cooking, it works well in herb butters and with eggs and cheese.

CHIVES A grasslike herb that produces a beautiful purplish flower. Its flavor resembles that of mild onions.

CILANTRO Huge bundles of fresh cilantro are a familiar sight in eastern Mediterranean markets, their warm, pungent aroma rising at the merest touch. The leaves impart a distinctive flavor to soups, stews, sauces and spicy dishes when added toward the end of cooking. They are also used sparingly in salads and yogurt dishes.

DILL Feathery dill leaves have a mild anise taste, popular in the eastern Mediterranean, particularly Greece and Turkey. It is chopped into fish and chicken dishes as well as stuffings and rice. Pickled gherkins and cucumbers are often flavored with dill.

MARJORAM A versatile herb of which there are several varieties. It grows both wild and cultivated and goes very well with red meats, game and tomato dishes. Oregano is a wild form of marjoram.

Basket of herbs

MINT One of the oldest and most widely used herbs. In Greece, chopped mint accompanies other herbs to enhance stuffed vegetables and fish dishes, and in Turkey and the Middle East, finely chopped mint adds a cooling tang to yogurt dishes as well as teas and iced drinks.

PARSLEY Flat-leaf parsley is far more widely used in Mediterranean cooking than the tightly curled variety. Mixed with garlic and lemon zest, it makes a wonderfully aromatic gremolata a colorful, refreshing garnish for scattering over tomato and rice dishes.

ROSEMARY Cut from the pretty flowering shrub, rosemary grows well throughout the Mediterranean and is most widely used in meat cooking. Several sprigs, tucked under a roast chicken or lamb with plenty of garlic, impart an inviting warm, sweet flavor.

SAGE Native to the northern Mediterranean, soft, velvety sage leaves have a strong, distinctive flavor and should be used sparingly in meat and game dishes. Sage can be added to stuffings or panfried with squab and liver to give an interesting flavor.

TARRAGON Long, lank tarragon leaves have a very individual aroma and flavor, most widely appreciated in French cooking. It is used generously in egg and chicken dishes, and with salmon and trout. Tarragon-flavored vinegar makes a delicious ingredient in a good mayonnaise or bearnaise sauce.

THYME A few sprigs of hardy thyme add a warm, earthy flavor to slow-cooked meat and poultry dishes as well as to pâtés, marinades and vegetable dishes.

SPICES

CARDAMOM Usually associated with Indian cooking, the use of cardamom extends to the eastern Mediterranean. The black, green or white pods should be pounded to release the small black seeds, which can be bruised to accentuate the flavor. The pods are usually discarded.

CHILES These are the small, fiery relatives of the sweet pepper family. Mediterranean chiles are generally milder in flavor than the fiery South American ones, but should still be used with caution, because their heat is difficult to gauge. It is the oil in chiles that accounts for the heat and the irritation they can cause to sensitive skin.

CINNAMON Cinnamon sticks, the thin curled bark of the cinnamon tree, have an aromatic, sweet flavor that is used extensively in the eastern Mediterranean to flavor meat and pilaf dishes and to infuse milk and syrups for desserts. Ground cinnamon is more convenient but lacks the fresh, sweet flavor.

CORIANDER SEEDS These seeds of the herb cilantro have a warm, slightly orange flavor that is essential to many dishes of the eastern Mediterranean. Their flavor can be accentuated by crushing and gently heating them in a frying pan before using.

CUMIN SEEDS These dark, spindly seeds are often married with coriander when making spicy dishes that are typical of North Africa and the eastern Mediterranean.

MACE This is the thin, lacy covering of nutmeg, available ground to a powder or as thin "blades." It has a gentler flavor than nutmeg.

NUTMEG Nutmeg's beautiful, sweet, warm aroma makes a good addition to sweet and savory dishes, particularly terrines and pâtés and those featuring spinach, cheese and eggs.

PEPPER There are several different types of peppercorns, all of which are picked from the pepper vine, a plant unrelated to the capsicum family. Black peppercorns have the strongest flavor. Green peppercorns are the fresh unripe berries, which are bottled while soft.

Preserved lemons

SAFFRON This is by far the most highly prized spice, since it takes the handpicked stamens of about 70,000 saffron crocuses to make up one pound of the spice. Its exotic, rich color and flavor are indispensable in many Mediterranean dishes, particularly French fish stews, Spanish rice and chicken dishes and Italian risottos. To accentuate the flavor, the strands should be lightly crushed and soaked in a little boiling water before use.

FLAVORINGS

CAPERS Capers are the pickled buds of a shrub native to the Mediterranean region. The best are those preserved in salt rather than brine or vinegar. When capers are coarsely chopped, their sharp piquant tang is used to cut the richness of lamb, liven up fish sauces and flavor salads and pastes such as tapenade.

GARLIC Sold in "braids" or as separate bulbs, the main consideration when buying garlic is that the cloves are plump and firm. Garlic is one of the most vital ingredients in Mediterranean cooking, and there are few recipes in which it would be out of place. Used crushed, sliced or even whole, garlic develops a smooth, gentle flavor with long, slow cooking. Used raw in salads, mayonnaise and sauces, garlic has a hot, fierce impact.

HARISSA A fiery-hot paste used mostly in North African cooking, it is made from a blend of chiles, garlic, cumin, coriander and cayenne and can be bought in small jars.

HONEY An ancient sweetener that depends on the flowers on which the bees have fed for its individual fragrance and flavor. The Turks and Greeks use it in their syrupy pastries and puddings, and small quantities are added to some savory dishes.

LEMONS AND LIMES The grated zest or squeezed juice of lemons and limes is widely added to fish, meat and poultry for a typically fresh flavor.

ORANGES Thinly pared strips of orange zest give a fresh fragrance, particularly in the fish stews and soups of southern France.

PRESERVED LEMONS AND LIMES Lemons or limes preserved in salt develop a mellow flavor and are much used in Mediterranean dishes. To make them, scrub and quarter almost through to the base and rub cut sides with salt. Pack tightly into a large sterilized jar. Half-fill the jar with more salt, adding some bay leaves, peppercorns and cinnamon if desired. Cover completely with lemon juice. Cover with a lid and store for two weeks, shaking the jar daily. Add a little olive oil to seal and use within one to six months, washing off the salt before use.

ROSE WATER This distilled essence of rose petals is used mainly in eastern Mediterranean desserts, giving a mild rose fragrance and flavor. The strength varies greatly, so add carefully at first.

TAHINI A smooth oily paste ground from sesame seeds and used to give a nutty flavor to Middle Eastern dishes.

TOMATO PASTE A concentrated paste made from fresh tomatoes, perfect for boosting the flavor of bland tomatoes in soups, stews and sauces. Use sun-dried tomato paste for a richer flavor.

OLIVE OIL

Besides its healthy qualities, olive oil is indispensable to Mediterranean cooking for its fine flavor. Italy, France and Spain produce some of the best. The richest oil comes from the first cold pressing of the olives, producing an aromatic green "virgin" oil.

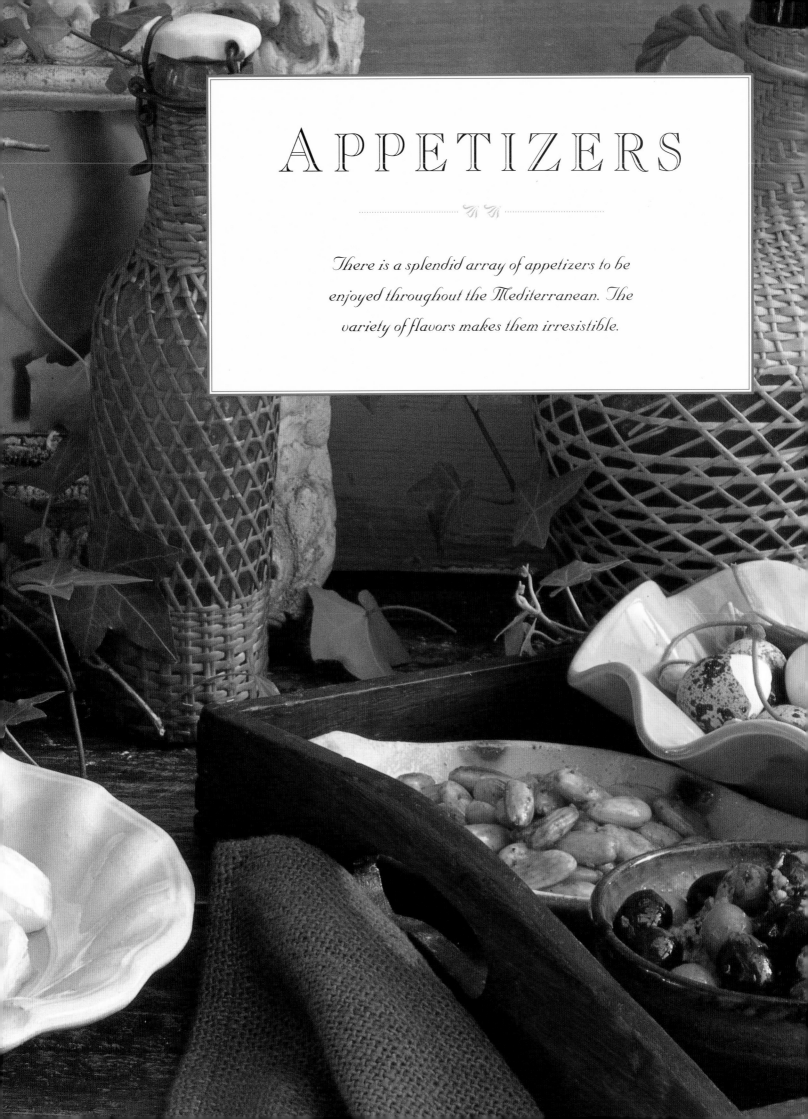

APPETIZERS

There is a splendid array of appetizers to be enjoyed throughout the Mediterranean. The variety of flavors makes them irresistible.

Tapas, apéritifs, mezze, mezedes—all these terms describe the inexhaustible and highly flavored range of appetizers that are served with drinks before a meal or as a light snack at almost any time of day. This is one of the most enticing aspects of Mediterranean cooking—the irresistible nibbles enjoyed in a casual, unhurried atmosphere, offering a culinary glimpse of the good things to follow. For the cook, the preparation of these savories can be as simple or as demanding as time and circumstances allow. Whether it is a selection of marinated olives, regional cheeses or fresh seafood or, on a more elaborate scale, delicious baked vegetables, pickles and spicy pastries, this informal style of enjoying food is quintessentially Mediterranean.

In Spanish, "tapa" means a lid, and it was the custom

RIGHT: Bent double, Moroccan farmworkers bring in the olive harvest.

LEFT: On the mountainous Greek island of Naxos, arable land is precious, and hillsides are extensively terraced.

of bartenders to serve glasses of sherry covered with a slice of bread topped with sausage or ham that evolved into the fascinating and imaginative selection of "little dishes" served today. Tapas bars, particularly abundant in southern Spain, serve a variety of such dishes. In these bars you can enjoy predinner bites or thoroughly indulge yourself with a selection of dishes as a main meal. Fried new potatoes, chorizo sausage in olive oil, garlic shrimp and empanadillas are tapas classics. The tortilla, an omelet in which fried potatoes are layered in a pan, covered with beaten eggs and baked to a set "cake," is another well-established dish. It is served warm or cold, cut into wedges, and washed down with local chilled wines or, like other tapas, with sherry, port or beer.

In the eastern Mediterranean, in places like Turkey, Greece, Lebanon and North Africa, local and specialized variations of mezze are popular with both locals and visitors. Arak, raki and ouzo, as well as wine, are drunk with a wonderful selection of foods to whet the appetite. These are usually highly spiced and aromatic. In Greece, sheep's and goat's milk yogurt are strained to produce thickened cheeses that are preserved in spiced olive oil. Spread on warm toast, this delicious snack is good

ABOVE: With his scales at the ready, a Turkish fisherman sets out his catch on his stall.

enough to enjoy as a complete meal. Stuffed tomatoes, fried halloumi or keflotyri cheese drizzled with lemon juice and pepper and a bowl of garlic-flavored Greek yogurt complete a mouthwatering spread.

Vegetables, salads and beans feature prominently in North African or Lebanese mezze. Simple vegetable crudités such as carrots, turnips and cucumber are scattered with coarse salt and left to marinate lightly before being moistened with lemon juice or wine vinegar. Miniature versions of national dishes such as kibbeh and little phyllo pastries are also ideal for whetting the appetite.

Sampling a selection of nibbles before a Turkish meal is almost compulsory, and the range of dishes is very extensive. A rich, thick sauce of tomato and chile and a refreshing cacik, or cucumber and yogurt salad, provide a stimulating contrast alongside specialties such as garlic mussels, broiled vegetables and stuffed bell peppers.

The classic Italian appetizer is the antipasto, usually an assortment of salami, prosciutto and other cured meats, served alongside roasted bell pepper salads, artichokes in olive oil, green bean vinaigrette, anchovy fillets and breads such as crostini and focaccia.

Tasty dips like tapenade, herb aïoli and a very garlicky vinaigrette are essential appetizers in France, often accompanied by a selection of raw or roasted crudités, herb salads and radishes with salt and butter.

Part of the pleasure of serving appetizers is that they can be as simple or as complicated as desired. Serve several as a light summer meal, two or three as a simple appetizer or a varied selection for a larger party. Added interest can be provided, with little extra effort, by serving a variety of olives, interesting Mediterranean breads and salted or spiced nuts.

Essentially, plenty of time must be allowed so that the nibbles can be enjoyed in the unhurried and relaxed atmosphere that is an integral part of the Mediterranean way of life.

DEEP-FRIED NEW POTATOES WITH SAFFRON AIOLI

Aïoli is a well-known garlic mayonnaise from Southern France; this Spanish version is very similiar.
In this recipe, saffron adds color and flavor.

1 egg yolk
½ teaspoon Dijon mustard
1¼ cups extra virgin olive oil
1–2 tablespoons lemon juice
1 garlic clove, crushed
½ teaspoon saffron strands
20 very small new potatoes
vegetable oil for frying
salt and ground black pepper

SERVES 4

1 To make the aïoli, put the egg yolk in a bowl with the mustard and a pinch of salt. Beat together with a wooden spoon. Still beating, add the olive oil very slowly, drop by drop to begin with, then, as the aïoli gradually thickens, in a thin stream. Add the lemon juice and salt and pepper to taste, then beat in the crushed garlic.

2 Place the saffron in a small bowl, and add 2 teaspoons hot water. Press the saffron with the back of a teaspoon to extract the color and flavor, and let infuse for about 5 minutes. Beat the saffron and the liquid into the mayonnaise.

3 Cook the potatoes in boiling salted water for 5 minutes, then turn off the heat. Cover the pan and let sit for 15 minutes. Drain the potatoes, then dry them thoroughly.

4 Heat ½ inch oil in a deep pan. When the oil is very hot, add the potatoes and fry quickly, turning, until crisp and golden. Drain on paper towels and serve with the saffron aïoli.

DATES STUFFED WITH CHORIZO

A delicious combination from Spain, using fresh dates and spicy chorizo sausage.

2 ounces chorizo sausage
12 fresh dates, pitted
6 bacon slices
oil for frying
flour for dusting
1 egg, beaten
1 cup fresh bread crumbs
toothpicks for serving

SERVES 4–6

1 Trim the ends of the chorizo sausage and peel away the skin. Cut into three ¾-inch slices. Cut these in half lengthwise, then into quarters, giving 12 pieces.

2 Stuff each date with a piece of chorizo, closing the date around it. Stretch the bacon by running the back of a knife along each slice. Cut each slice in half crosswise. Wrap a piece of bacon around each date and secure with a toothpick.

3 In a deep pan, heat ½ inch of oil. Dust the dates with flour, dip them in the beaten egg, then coat in bread crumbs. Fry the dates in the hot oil, turning them, until golden. Remove the dates with a slotted spoon and drain on paper towels. Serve immediately.

SPINACH EMPANADILLAS

These are little pastry turnovers, filled with ingredients that show a strong Moorish influence—pine nuts and raisins.

2 tablespoons raisins
1½ tablespoons olive oil
1 pound fresh spinach, washed
and chopped
6 drained canned anchovies, chopped
2 garlic cloves, finely chopped
⅓ cup pine nuts, chopped
1 egg, beaten
12 ounces puff pastry
salt and ground black pepper

MAKES 20

1 To make the filling, soak the raisins in a little warm water for 10 minutes. Drain, then chop them coarsely. Heat the oil in a large sauté pan or wok, add the spinach, stir, then cover and cook over low heat for about 2 minutes. Uncover, turn up the heat and let any liquid evaporate. Add the anchovies, garlic and seasoning. Cook, stirring, for another minute. Remove from the heat, add the raisins and pine nuts, and cool.

2 Preheat the oven to 350°F. On a floured surface, roll out the pastry to a ⅛-inch thickness.

3 Using a 3-inch pastry cutter, cut out 20 circles, re-rolling the dough if necessary. Place about 2 teaspoons of the filling in the middle of each circle, then brush the edges with a little water. Bring up the sides of the pastry and seal well (*left*). Press the edges together with the back of a fork. Brush with egg. Place the turnovers on a lightly greased baking sheet and bake for about 15 minutes, until golden. Serve warm.

SAUTEED MUSSELS WITH GARLIC AND HERBS

These mussels are served without their shells, in a delicious paprika-flavored sauce.
Eat them with toothpicks.

2 pounds fresh mussels
1 lemon slice
6 tablespoons olive oil
2 shallots, finely chopped
1 garlic clove, finely chopped
1 tablespoon chopped fresh parsley
½ teaspoon sweet paprika
¼ teaspoon dried red pepper flakes
parsley sprigs, to garnish

SERVES 4

1 Scrub the mussels, discarding any damaged ones that do not close when tapped with a knife. Put the mussels in a large pan with 1 cup water and the slice of lemon. Bring to a boil and let boil for 3–4 minutes, removing the mussels as they open. Discard any that remain closed. Take the mussels out of the shells and drain them on paper towels.

2 Heat the oil in a sauté pan, add the mussels *(left)* and cook, stirring, for a minute. Remove from the pan. Add the shallots and garlic and cook, covered, over low heat for about 5 minutes, until soft. Stir in the parsley, paprika and red pepper flakes, then add the mussels with any juices. Cook briefly. Remove the pan from the heat, cover and let sit for 1–2 minutes to let the flavors mingle. Serve, garnished with parsley.

TAPAS OF ALMONDS, OLIVES AND CHEESE

These three simple ingredients are lightly flavored to create a delicious Spanish tapas medley that's perfect for a casual appetizer or nibbles to serve with cocktails.

FOR THE MARINATED OLIVES
½ teaspoon coriander seeds
½ teaspoon fennel seeds
1 teaspoon chopped fresh rosemary
2 teaspoons chopped fresh parsley
2 garlic cloves, crushed
1 tablespoon sherry vinegar
2 tablespoons olive oil
⅔ cup black olives
⅔ cup green olives

FOR THE MARINATED CHEESE
5 ounces goat cheese, or Spanish sheep's milk cheese
6 tablespoons olive oil
1 tablespoon white wine vinegar
1 teaspoon black peppercorns
1 garlic clove, sliced
3 fresh tarragon or thyme sprigs
tarragon sprigs, to garnish

FOR THE SALTED ALMONDS
¼ teaspoon cayenne pepper
2 tablespoons sea salt
2 tablespoons butter
4 tablespoons olive oil
1¾ cups blanched almonds
extra salt for sprinkling (optional)

SERVES 6–8

1 To make the marinated olives, crush the coriander and fennel seeds with a mortar and pestle. Combine with the rosemary, parsley, garlic, vinegar and oil and pour over the olives in a small bowl. Cover and chill for up to 1 week.

2 To make the marinated cheese, cut the cheese into bite-size pieces, leaving the rind on. Combine the oil, vinegar, peppercorns, garlic and herb sprigs and pour over the cheese in a small bowl. Cover and chill for up to 3 days.

COOK'S TIP
If serving with cocktails, provide toothpicks for spearing the olives and cheese.

3 To make the salted almonds, combine the cayenne pepper and salt in a bowl. Melt the butter with the olive oil in a frying pan. Add the almonds to the pan and fry, stirring, for about 5 minutes, until the almonds are golden.

4 Pour the almonds out of the frying pan into the salt mixture and toss together until the almonds are coated. Let cool, then store them in a jar or airtight container for up to 1 week.

5 To serve the tapas, arrange in small, shallow serving dishes. Use fresh sprigs of tarragon to garnish the cheese and sprinkle a little more salt on the almonds, if desired.

ROASTED BELL PEPPER ANTIPASTO

Jars of Italian mixed peppers in olive oil are now a common sight in many supermarkets. None, however, can compete with this colorful, freshly made version, perfect as an appetizer on its own, or with some Italian salamis and cold meats.

3 red bell peppers
2 yellow or orange bell peppers
2 green bell peppers
½ cup sun-dried tomatoes in oil, drained
2 tablespoons balsamic vinegar
5 tablespoons olive oil
few drops of hot pepper sauce
4 canned artichoke hearts, drained and sliced
1 garlic clove, sliced
salt and ground black pepper
basil leaves, to garnish

SERVES 6

1 Preheat the oven to 400°F. Lightly oil a foil-lined baking sheet and place the whole peppers on the foil. Bake for about 45 minutes, until beginning to char. Remove from the oven, cover with a dish towel and let cool for 5 minutes.

2 Slice the sun-dried tomatoes. Remove the core and seeds from the peppers and peel away the skins. Slice each pepper into thick strips.

3 Beat together the vinegar, oil and hot pepper sauce, then season with a little salt and pepper.

4 Toss the peppers with the sliced artichokes, tomatoes and garlic. Pour the dressing over and sprinkle the basil leaves on top.

FONDUTA

Fontina is a medium-fat Italian cheese with a rich salty flavor, a little like that of Gruyère, which makes a good substitute. This delicious cheese dip needs only some warm ciabatta or focaccia, an herb salad and some robust red wine to make a thoroughly enjoyable meal.

9 ounces fontina cheese, diced
1 cup milk
1 tablespoon butter
2 eggs, lightly beaten
ground black pepper

SERVES 4

1 Place the cheese in a bowl, add the milk and let soak for 2–3 hours. Transfer to a double boiler or a heatproof bowl set over a pan of simmering water.

2 Add the butter and eggs and cook gently, stirring, until the cheese has melted to a smooth sauce with the consistency of custard.

3 Remove from heat and transfer to a serving dish. Grind on some pepper and serve immediately.

COOK'S TIP
Don't overheat the sauce, or the eggs might curdle. Very gentle heat will produce a lovely, smooth sauce.

GARLIC SHRIMP

For this simple Spanish tapas dish, you really need fresh raw shrimp, which absorb the flavors of the garlic and chiles as they cook. Have everything ready for last-minute cooking so you can take the dish to the table still sizzling.

*12 ounces—1 pound large
raw shrimp
2 fresh red chiles
5 tablespoons olive oil
3 garlic cloves, crushed
salt and ground black pepper*

SERVES 4

1 Remove the heads and shells from the shrimp, leaving the tails intact.

2 Halve each chile lengthwise and discard the seeds. Heat the oil in a flameproof pan, suitable for serving. (Alternatively, use a frying pan and have a warmed serving dish ready in the oven.)

3 Add all the shrimp, chiles and garlic to the pan and cook over high heat for about 3 minutes, stirring, until the shrimp turn pink. Season lightly with salt and pepper and serve immediately.

CHORIZO IN OLIVE OIL

Spanish chorizo sausage has a deliciously pungent taste; its robust seasoning of garlic, chile and paprika flavors the ingredients it is cooked with. Frying chorizo with onions and olive oil is one of its simplest and most delicious uses.

*5 tablespoons extra virgin olive oil
12 ounces chorizo sausage, sliced
1 large onion, thinly sliced
coarsely chopped flat-leaf parsley,
to garnish*

SERVES 4

VARIATION
Chorizo is usually available in large supermarkets or delicatessens. Other similarly rich, spicy sausages can be used as a substitute.

1 Heat the oil in a frying pan and fry the chorizo sausage over high heat until beginning to color. Remove from pan with slotted spoon.

2 Add the onion to the pan and fry until colored. Return the sausage slices to the pan and heat through for 1 minute.

3 Pour the mixture into a shallow serving dish and sprinkle with the parsley. Serve with warm bread.

CROSTINI

These are Italian canapés, consisting of toasted slices of bread spread with various toppings. The following recipes are for a chicken liver pâté and a shrimp butter.

FOR THE CHICKEN LIVER PATE
10 tablespoons butter
1 small onion, finely chopped
1 garlic clove, crushed
8 ounces chicken livers
4 sage leaves, chopped
salt and ground black pepper

FOR THE SHRIMP BUTTER
8 ounces cooked, peeled shrimp
2 drained canned anchovies
4 tablespoons butter, softened
1 tablespoon lemon juice
1 tablespoon chopped fresh parsley
salt and ground black pepper

FOR THE CROSTINI
12 slices crusty Italian or French bread, cut ½-inch thick
6 tablespoons butter, melted

FOR THE GARNISH
sage leaves
flat-leaf parsley

SERVES 6

 To make the chicken liver pâté, melt half the butter in a frying pan, add the onion and garlic, and fry gently until soft. Add the chicken livers and sage and sauté for about 8 minutes, until the livers are brown and firm. Season with salt and pepper and process in a blender or food processor with the remaining butter.

 To make the shrimp butter, chop the shrimp and anchovies finely. Place in a bowl with the butter and beat together until well blended. Add the lemon juice and parsley and season with salt and pepper. Preheat the oven to 400°F. Place the bread slices on one or two baking sheets and brush with the butter.

3 Bake for 8–10 minutes, until pale golden. Spread half the hot crostini with the pâté and the rest with the shrimp butter, garnishing with sage and parsley, respectively. Serve the crostini immediately.

COOK'S TIP
Both the chicken liver pâté and the shrimp butter can be made ahead, but should be used within two days. Cover both toppings tightly and store them in the refrigerator.

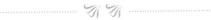

MARINATED BABY EGGPLANT WITH RAISINS AND PINE NUTS

Eggplant is popular in all the Mediterranean countries. This is a recipe with an Italian influence, using ingredients that have been included in recipes since Renaissance times. Make a day in advance, to let the sweet and sour flavors develop.

12 baby eggplant, halved lengthwise
1 cup extra virgin olive oil
juice of 1 lemon
2 tablespoons balsamic vinegar
3 cloves
⅓ cup pine nuts
2 tablespoons raisins
1 tablespoon sugar
1 bay leaf
large pinch of dried red pepper flakes
salt and ground black pepper

SERVES 4

1 Preheat the broiler to high. Place the eggplant, cut side up, in the broiler pan and brush with a little of the olive oil. Broil for about 10 minutes, until slightly blackened, turning them over halfway through cooking.

2 To make the marinade, put the remaining olive oil, the lemon juice, vinegar, cloves, pine nuts, raisins, sugar and bay leaf in a bowl. Add the red pepper flakes and salt and pepper and mix well.

3 Place the hot eggplant in an earthenware or glass bowl, and pour the marinade over. Let cool, turning the eggplant once or twice. Serve cold.

YOGURT CHEESE IN OLIVE OIL

Sheep's milk is widely used in cheese making in the eastern Mediterranean, particularly in Greece, where sheep's milk yogurt is hung in cheesecloth to drain off the whey before being patted into balls of soft cheese. Here it's preserved in olive oil with chiles and herbs—an appropriate gift for a "foodie" friend.

1¾ pounds sheep's milk yogurt
½ teaspoon salt
2 teaspoons crushed dried chiles or chili powder
1 tablespoon chopped fresh rosemary
1 tablespoon chopped fresh thyme or oregano
1¼ cups olive oil, preferably garlic-flavored

FILLS TWO 1-POUND JARS

1 Sterilize a 12-inch square of cheesecloth by steeping it in boiling water. Drain and lay over a large plate. Mix the yogurt with the salt and pour onto the center of the cheesecloth. Bring up the sides of the cheesecloth and tie firmly with string.

2 Hang the bag on a kitchen cupboard handle or suitable position where the bag can be suspended with a bowl underneath to catch the whey. Leave for 2–3 days until the yogurt stops dripping.

3 Sterilize two 1-pound glass preserving or jam jars by heating them in the oven at 300°F for 15 minutes.

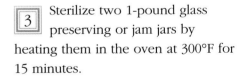

4 Combine the chiles and herbs. Take teaspoonfuls of the cheese and roll into balls with your hands. Lower into the jars, sprinkling each layer with the herb mixture.

5   Pour the oil over the cheese until completely covered. Store in the refrigerator for up to 3 weeks.

6   To serve the cheese, spoon out of the jars with a little of the flavored olive oil and spread on lightly toasted bread.

COOK'S TIP

If your kitchen is particularly warm, find a cooler place to suspend the cheese. Alternatively, drain the cheese in the refrigerator, suspending the bag from one of the shelves.

TAPENADE AND HERB AÏOLI WITH SUMMER VEGETABLES

A beautiful platter of salad vegetables served with one or two interesting sauces makes a thoroughly delicious and informal appetizer. This colorful French dish is perfect for entertaining, as it can be prepared in advance.

FOR THE TAPENADE
1½ cups pitted black olives
2-ounce can anchovy fillets, drained
2 tablespoons capers
½ cup olive oil
finely grated zest of 1 lemon
1 tablespoon brandy (optional)
ground black pepper

FOR THE HERB AÏOLI
2 egg yolks
1 teaspoon Dijon mustard
2 teaspoons white wine vinegar
1 cup light olive oil
3 tablespoons chopped mixed fresh
herbs, such as chervil, parsley
or tarragon
2 tablespoons chopped watercress
5 garlic cloves, crushed
salt and ground black pepper

TO SERVE
2 red bell peppers, seeded and cut into
wide strips
2 tablespoons olive oil
8 ounces new potatoes
4 ounces green beans
8 ounces baby carrots
8 ounces young asparagus
12 quail's eggs (optional)
fresh herbs, to garnish
coarse salt for sprinkling

SERVES 6

1 To make the tapenade, finely chop the olives, anchovies and capers and beat together with the oil, lemon zest and brandy if using. (Alternatively, lightly process the ingredients in a blender or food processor, scraping down the mixture from the sides of the bowl if necessary.)

2 Season with pepper and blend in a little more oil if the mixture is very dry. Transfer to a serving dish.

3 To make the aïoli, beat together the egg yolks, mustard and vinegar. Gradually blend in the oil, a trickle at a time, whisking well after each addition until thick and smooth. Season with salt and pepper to taste, adding a little more vinegar if the aïoli tastes bland.

4 Stir in the mixed herbs, watercress and garlic, then transfer to a serving dish. Cover and put in the refrigerator.

5 Put the peppers on a foil-lined broiler rack and brush with the oil. Broil under high heat until just beginning to char.

6 Cook the potatoes in a large pan of boiling salted water until just tender. Add the beans and carrots and cook for 1 minute. Add the asparagus and cook for another 30 seconds. Drain the vegetables.

7 Cook the quail's eggs (if using) in boiling water for 2 minutes. Drain and remove half of each shell.

8 Arrange all the vegetables, eggs and sauces on a serving platter. Garnish with fresh herbs and serve with coarse salt for sprinkling.

COOK'S TIP
Keep any leftover sauces for serving with salads. The tapenade is also delicious tossed with pasta or spread on warm toast.

BROILED VEGETABLE TERRINE

—

A colorful layered terrine, using vegetables associated with the Mediterranean.

2 large red bell peppers, quartered,
cored and seeded
2 large yellow bell peppers, quartered,
cored and seeded
1 large eggplant, sliced lengthwise
2 large zucchini, sliced lengthwise
6 tablespoons olive oil
1 large red onion, thinly sliced
½ cup raisins
1 tablespoon tomato paste
1 tablespoon red wine vinegar
1⅔ cups tomato juice
2 tablespoons powdered gelatin
fresh basil leaves, to garnish

FOR THE DRESSING
6 tablespoons extra virgin olive oil
2 tablespoons red wine vinegar
salt and ground black pepper

SERVES 6

1 Place the prepared red and yellow peppers skin side up under a hot broiler and cook until the skins are blackened. Transfer to a bowl and cover with a plate. Let cool.

2 Arrange the eggplant and zucchini slices on separate baking sheets. Brush them with a little oil and cook under the broiler, turning occasionally, until tender and golden.

3 Heat the remaining olive oil in a frying pan and add the sliced onion, raisins, tomato paste and red wine vinegar. Cook gently until soft and syrupy. Let the mixture cool in the frying pan.

4 Line a 7½-cup terrine with plastic wrap (it helps to oil the terrine lightly first), leaving a little hanging over the sides.

5 Pour half the tomato juice into a saucepan and sprinkle with the gelatin. Dissolve gently over low heat, stirring.

6 Place a layer of red peppers in the bottom of the terrine and pour in enough of the tomato juice with gelatin to cover. Continue layering the eggplant, zucchini, yellow peppers and onion mixture, finishing with another layer of red peppers. Pour tomato juice over each layer of vegetables.

7 Add the remaining tomato juice to any left in the pan, and pour into the terrine. Give it a sharp tap, to disperse the juice. Cover the terrine and chill until set.

8 To make the dressing, whisk together the oil and vinegar and season with salt and pepper. Turn out the terrine and remove the plastic wrap. Serve in thick slices, drizzled with dressing. Garnish with basil leaves.

SOUPS

❧ ❧

*Soups are a vital part of the culinary heritage of
the Mediterranean. From winter warmers to
summer coolers, there's a soup for every season.*

Soups have long been an important part of the Mediterranean diet. In the past, when a lot of the countries were poverty-stricken, soup constituted a meal for many. These broths were made with dried beans, peas and lentils, particularly during the cold winter months. Eaten with plenty of bread, they were filling and provided nourishment. Fresh vegetables were added in season, and sometimes eggs. Many of these soups, therefore, were extremely simple. Some of the recipes that exist today have been passed down through the generations, only to be given new life, and new status, with the rising popularity of "peasant food" in restaurants and cookbooks. These are unfussy recipes, which rely for their success on the quality of the ingredients. Take garlic soup, for example, which is made in various ways throughout Spain and France; in its simplest form, it is nothing but garlic, water and seasoning, but with the best garlic, these basic ingredients are transformed into a delicious and fragrant liquor. This basic method is applied to many vegetables, with the water sometimes replaced with a meat stock, and the mixture sometimes put through a strainer, to produce a smooth soup.

Pumpkins, Jerusalem artichokes, tomatoes, bell peppers,

asparagus and spinach are just a few of the many varieties of vegetables used to make soup.

Soups containing meat are usually hearty, combined as they are with pulses such as lentils or chickpeas, or potatoes, rice or pasta. In the Middle East, beef and lamb are used, and soups are seasoned with spices and herbs. There are special feast day soups, and soups to eat after sunset during the fast of Ramadan. However, the more typical Mediterranean soup is based on vegetables, beans,

ABOVE: *Dawn in Corfu, and a fisherman prepares to head out to sea.*

and of course, fish and shellfish. Wonderful fish soups come in numerous different guises; the now famous, and often poorly imitated, bouillabaisse is a "stew" of various varieties of fish and seafood native to the coast of the south of France. The dish originated in the port of Marseilles. Again, these soups serve as complete meals, sometimes with the fish and broth offered separately, accompanied by bread or toasted croutons.

Every country and coastal region has its own specialty, and the soup will never be quite the same, the ingredients depending on the fishermen's catch that day. Many of the recipes were originated by the fishermen themselves, who cooked them on their boats, using fish that they couldn't sell in the market, because it had no commercial value. Today, with a wide choice of fish available in fish stores and supermarkets, it is possible to re-cre-

ate many of these wonderful dishes at home.

Chilled soups come from the south of Spain, where gazpacho is extremely popular—this is a delicious and refreshing mixture of raw tomatoes, bell peppers and cucumbers, which makes the perfect lunch for a hot summer day. Again, there are variations on this classic recipe, with such diverse ingredients as almonds and grapes. Cold soups are also featured in the Middle East—these are yogurt-based, usually mixed with cucumber and garlic, spiked with mint.

Tourists who travel to the Mediterranean seldom sample more than a few of the many different soups available, but it is worth investigating that delicious smell wafting from a restaurant kitchen, or asking the name of the delectable-looking soup that is being enjoyed at the next table.

Changing at the whim of the cook, or to take best advantage of the finest market produce, Mediterranean soups are certainly a cause for celebration.

BOUILLABAISSE

Perhaps the most famous of all Mediterranean fish soups, this dish, originating in Marseilles in the south of France, is a rich and colorful mixture of fish and shellfish, flavored with tomatoes, saffron and orange.

3–3½ pounds mixed fish and raw
shellfish, such as red mullet, porgy,
monkfish, red snapper,
whiting, large shrimp and clams
8 ounces ripe tomatoes
pinch of saffron strands
6 tablespoons olive oil
1 onion, sliced
1 leek, sliced
1 celery stalk, sliced
2 garlic cloves, crushed
1 bouquet garni
1 strip pared orange zest
½ teaspoon fennel seeds
1 tablespoon tomato paste
2 teaspoons Pernod
4–6 thick slices French bread
3 tablespoons chopped fresh parsley
salt and ground black pepper

SERVES 4–6

2 Cut the fish into large chunks. Leave the shellfish in their shells. Scald the tomatoes, then drain and refresh in cold water. Peel and coarsely chop them. Soak the saffron in 1–2 tablespoons hot water.

3 Heat the oil in a large pan, add the onion, leek and celery and cook until softened. Add the garlic, bouquet garni, orange zest, fennel seeds and tomatoes, then stir in the saffron and liquid and the fish stock. Season with salt and pepper, then bring to a boil and simmer for 30–40 minutes.

4 Add the shellfish and boil for about 6 minutes. Add the fish and cook for another 6–8 minutes, until it flakes easily.

5 Using a slotted spoon, transfer the fish to a warmed serving platter. Keep the liquid boiling, to allow the oil to emulsify with the broth. Add the tomato paste and Pernod, then check the seasoning. To serve, place a slice of French bread in each soup bowl, pour the broth on top and serve the fish and shellfish separately, sprinkled with the parsley.

1 Remove the heads, tails and fins from the fish and put them in a large pan with about 5 cups water. Bring to a boil and simmer for 15 minutes. Strain, reserving the liquid.

CHILLED ALMOND SOUP

Unless you want to spend time pounding the ingredients for this dish by hand, a food processor is essential.
Then you'll find that this Spanish soup is very simple to make and refreshing to eat on a hot day.

2 slices fresh white bread
1 cup blanched almonds
2 garlic cloves, sliced
5 tablespoons olive oil
1½ tablespoons sherry vinegar
salt and ground black pepper
toasted sliced almonds and
seedless green and black grapes,
halved and peeled, to garnish

SERVES 6

1 Break the bread into a bowl and pour ⅔ cup cold water over it. Let sit for 5 minutes.

2 Put the blanched almonds and garlic in a blender or food processor and process until very finely ground. Blend in the soaked bread.

3 Gradually add the olive oil until the mixture forms a smooth paste. Add the sherry vinegar, then 2½ cups cold water, and process until smooth.

4 Transfer to a bowl and season with salt and pepper, adding a little more water if the soup is very thick. Chill for at least 2–3 hours.

5 Ladle the soup into bowls and sprinkle with the toasted almonds and peeled grapes.

GAZPACHO

There are many versions of this refreshingly chilled, pungent soup from southern Spain. All contain an intense blend of tomatoes, peppers, cucumber and garlic, perfect on a hot summer's evening.

2 pounds ripe tomatoes
1 cucumber
2 red bell peppers, seeded and
coarsely chopped
2 garlic cloves, crushed
3 cups fresh white bread crumbs
2 tablespoons white wine vinegar
2 tablespoons sun-dried tomato paste
6 tablespoons olive oil
salt and ground black pepper

To finish
1 slice white bread, crust removed
and cut into cubes
2 tablespoons olive oil
6–12 ice cubes
small bowl of mixed chopped
garnishes, such as tomato, cucumber,
red onion, hard-boiled egg and flat-
leaf parsley or tarragon leaves

Serves 6

Cook's Tip
The sun-dried tomato paste has been added to accentuate the flavor of the tomatoes. You might not need this if you use a really flavorful variety.

2 Process half the mixture in a blender or food processor until fairly smooth. Process the remaining mixture and combine with the first.

3 Check the seasoning and add a little cold water if the soup is too thick. Chill for several hours.

1 Plunge the tomatoes into boiling water for 30 seconds, then refresh in cold water. Peel away the skins and quarter. Peel and coarsely chop the cucumber. Mix the tomatoes and cucumber in a bowl with the peppers, garlic, bread crumbs, vinegar, tomato paste and olive oil and season lightly with salt and pepper.

4 To finish, fry the bread in the oil until golden. Spoon the soup into bowls, adding one or two ice cubes to each. Serve accompanied by the croutons and garnishes.

SPICED MUSSEL SOUP

Chunky and colorful, this Turkish fish soup is like a chowder in its consistency. It's flavored with harissa, a spicy paste more familiar in North African cooking.

3–3½ pounds fresh mussels
⅔ cup white wine
3 tomatoes
2 tablespoons olive oil
1 onion, finely chopped
2 garlic cloves, crushed
2 celery stalks, thinly sliced
bunch of scallions, thinly sliced
1 potato, diced
1½ teaspoons harissa
3 tablespoons chopped fresh parsley
ground black pepper
thick yogurt, to serve (optional)

SERVES 6

1 Scrub the mussels, discarding any damaged ones or any open ones that do not close when tapped with a knife.

2 Bring the wine to a boil in a large saucepan. Add the mussels and cover with a lid. Cook for 4–5 minutes, until the mussels have opened wide. Discard any mussels that remain closed. Drain the mussels, reserving the cooking liquid. Reserve a few mussels in their shells for garnish and shell the rest.

3 Peel the tomatoes and dice them. Heat the oil in a pan and sauté the onion, garlic, celery and scallions for 5 minutes.

4 Add the shelled mussels, reserved liquid, potato, harissa and tomatoes. Bring just to a boil, reduce the heat and cover. Simmer gently for 25 minutes or until the potatoes are breaking up.

5 Stir in the parsley and pepper and add the reserved mussels. Heat through for 1 minute. Serve hot, with a spoonful of yogurt, if desired.

GREEN LENTIL SOUP

Lentil soup is an eastern Mediterranean classic, varying in its spiciness according to region. Red or puy lentils make equally good substitutes for the green lentils used here.

1 cup green lentils
5 tablespoons olive oil
3 onions, finely chopped
2 garlic cloves, thinly sliced
2 teaspoons cumin seeds, crushed
¼ teaspoon ground turmeric
2½ cups chicken or vegetable stock
salt and ground black pepper
2 tablespoons coarsely chopped
chopped cilantro

SERVES 4–6

1 Put the lentils in a saucepan and cover with cold water. Bring to a boil and boil rapidly for 10 minutes. Drain.

2 Heat 2 tablespoons of the oil in a pan and sauté two-thirds of the chopped onions with the garlic, cumin and turmeric for 3 minutes, stirring. Add the lentils, stock and 2½ cups water. Bring to a boil, reduce the heat, cover and simmer gently for 30 minutes, until the lentils are soft.

3 Sauté the remaining onion in the remaining oil until golden.

4 Use a potato masher to lightly mash the lentils and make the soup pulpy. Reheat gently and season with salt and pepper to taste. Pour the soup into bowls. Stir the chopped cilantro into the sautéed onion and sprinkle on the soup. Serve with warm bread.

MOROCCAN HARIRA

This is a hearty meat and vegetable soup, eaten during the month of Ramadan, when the Muslim population fasts between sunrise and sunset.

1 pound ripe tomatoes
½ pound lamb, cut into ½-inch pieces
½ teaspoon ground turmeric
½ teaspoon ground cinnamon
2 tablespoons butter
4 tablespoons chopped cilantro
2 tablespoons chopped fresh parsley
1 onion, chopped
¼ cup split red lentils
½ cup dried chickpeas, soaked overnight
4 baby onions or small shallots, peeled
¼ cup soup noodles
salt and ground black pepper
chopped fresh cilantro, lemon slices and ground cinnamon, to garnish

SERVES 4

Put the lamb, turmeric, cinnamon, butter, cilantro, parsley and onion into a large pan, and cook over medium heat, stirring, for 5 minutes. Add the chopped tomatoes and continue to cook for 10 minutes.

Rinse the lentils under running water and add to the pan with the drained chickpeas and 2½ cups water. Season with salt and pepper. Bring to a boil, cover, and simmer gently for 1½ hours.

1 Plunge the tomatoes into boiling water for 30 seconds, then refresh in cold water. Peel away the skins. Cut into quarters and remove the seeds. Chop coarsely.

4 Add the onions and cook for another 30 minutes. Add the noodles 5 minutes before the end of the cooking time. Garnish with the cilantro, lemon slices and cinnamon.

RIBOLLITA

Ribollita is a lot like minestrone. In Italy it is traditionally served ladled over bread and a rich green vegetable, although you could omit this for a lighter version.

3 tablespoons olive oil
2 onions, chopped
2 carrots, sliced
4 garlic cloves, crushed
2 celery stalks, thinly sliced
1 fennel bulb, trimmed and chopped
2 large zucchini, thinly sliced
14-ounce can chopped tomatoes
2 tablespoons homemade or
store-bought pesto
3¾ cups vegetable stock
14-ounce can navy or pinto
beans, drained
salt and ground black pepper

TO FINISH
1 pound young spinach
1 tablespoon extra virgin olive oil, plus
extra for drizzling
6–8 slices crusty white bread
Parmesan cheese shavings

SERVES 6–8

VARIATION
Use other dark greens, such as chard or cabbage, instead of the spinach; shred and cook until tender.

1 Heat the oil in a large saucepan. Add the onions, carrots, garlic, celery and fennel and sauté gently for 10 minutes. Add the zucchini and sauté for another 2 minutes.

2 Add the chopped tomatoes, pesto, stock and beans and bring to a boil. Reduce the heat, cover and simmer gently for 25–30 minutes, until the vegetables are completely tender. Season with salt and pepper to taste.

3 To serve, sauté the spinach in the oil for 2 minutes or until wilted. Spoon over the bread in soup bowls, then ladle the soup over the spinach. Serve with extra olive oil for drizzling onto the soup and Parmesan cheese to sprinkle on top.

SEAFOOD SOUP WITH ROUILLE

This is a chunky, aromatic mixed fish soup from France, flavored with plenty of saffron and herbs.
Rouille, a fiery hot paste, is served separately for diners to swirl into their soup to flavor.

3 snapper or red mullet, scaled
and gutted
12 large shrimp
1½ pounds white fish, such as cod,
haddock, halibut or monkfish
½ pound fresh mussels
1 onion, quartered
1 teaspoon saffron strands
5 tablespoons olive oil
1 fennel bulb, coarsely chopped
4 garlic cloves, crushed
3 strips pared orange zest
4 thyme sprigs
1½ pounds tomatoes or 14-ounce can
chopped tomatoes
2 tablespoons sun-dried tomato paste
3 bay leaves
salt and ground black pepper

FOR THE ROUILLE
1 red bell pepper, seeded and
coarsely chopped
1 red chile, seeded and sliced
2 garlic cloves, chopped
5 tablespoons olive oil
¼ cup fresh bread crumbs

SERVES 6

2 | Fillet the snapper or mullet by cutting the flesh from either side of the backbone, reserving the heads and bones. Cut the fillets into small chunks. Shell half the shrimp and reserve the trimmings for the stock. Skin the white fish, discarding any bones, and cut into chunks. Thoroughly scrub the mussels, discarding any that are damaged or any open ones that do not close when tapped with a knife.

3 | Put the fish heads and bones and shrimp trimmings in a large saucepan with the onion and about 5 cups water. Bring to a boil, then simmer gently for 30 minutes. Cool slightly and strain.

4 | Soak the saffron in 1 tablespoon boiling water. Heat about 2 tablespoons of the oil in a large sauté pan or saucepan. Add the snapper or mullet and white fish and sauté over high heat for 1 minute. Drain.

5 | Heat the remaining oil and sauté the fennel, garlic, orange zest and thyme until beginning to color. Make up the strained stock to about 5 cups with water.

1 | To make the rouille, process the pepper, chile, garlic, oil and bread crumbs in a blender or food processor until smooth. Transfer to a serving dish and chill.

COOK'S TIP
To save time, order the fish and ask the fish seller to fillet the snapper or mullet for you.

6 | If using fresh tomatoes, plunge them into boiling water for 30 seconds, then refresh in cold water. Peel and chop. Add the stock to the pan with the saffron, tomatoes, tomato paste and bay leaves. Season, bring almost to a boil, then simmer gently, covered, for 20 minutes.

7 | Stir in the snapper or mullet, white fish and shrimp and add the mussels. Cover the pan and cook for 3–4 minutes. Discard any mussels that do not open. Serve the soup hot with the rouille.

SPICY PUMPKIN SOUP

Pumpkin is popular all over the Mediterranean, and it's an important ingredient in Middle Eastern cooking, by which this soup is inspired. Ginger and cumin give the soup its spicy flavor.

*2 pounds pumpkin, peeled and
seeds removed
2 tablespoons olive oil
2 leeks, trimmed and sliced
1 garlic clove, crushed
1 teaspoon ground ginger
1 teaspoon ground cumin
3¾ cups chicken stock
salt and ground black pepper
cilantro leaves, to garnish
4 tablespoons plain yogurt, to serve*

SERVES 4

1 Cut the pumpkin into chunks. Heat the oil in a large pan and add the leeks and garlic. Cook gently until softened.

2 Add the ginger and cumin and cook, stirring, for another minute. Add the pumpkin and the chicken stock and season with salt and pepper. Bring to a boil and simmer for 30 minutes, until the pumpkin is tender. Process the soup, in batches if necessary, in a blender or food processor.

3 Reheat the soup and serve in warmed individual bowls, with a swirl of yogurt and a garnish of cilantro leaves.

MIDDLE EASTERN YOGURT AND CUCUMBER SOUP

Yogurt is used extensively in Middle Eastern cooking, and it is usually made at home. Sometimes it is added at the end of cooking a dish, so that it won't curdle, but in this cold soup the yogurt is one of the basic ingredients.

1 large cucumber, peeled
1¼ cups light cream
⅔ cup plain yogurt
2 garlic cloves, crushed
2 tablespoons white wine vinegar
1 tablespoon chopped fresh mint
salt and ground black pepper
sprigs of mint, to garnish

SERVES 4

1 Grate the cucumber coarsely. Place in a bowl with the cream, yogurt, garlic, vinegar and mint. Stir well and season to taste.

2 Chill for at least 2 hours before serving. Just before serving, stir the soup again. Pour into individual bowls and garnish with mint sprigs.

55

PISTOU

A delicious vegetable soup from Nice in the south of France, served with a sun-dried tomato pesto and fresh Parmesan cheese.

1 zucchini, diced
1 small potato, diced
1 shallot, chopped
1 carrot, diced
8-ounce can chopped tomatoes
5 cups vegetable stock
2 ounces green beans, cut into
½-inch pieces
½ cup frozen tiny peas
½ cup small pasta shapes
4–6 tablespoons homemade or
bought pesto
1 tablespoon sun-dried tomato paste
salt and ground black pepper
freshly grated Parmesan cheese,
to serve

SERVES 4–6

1 Place the zucchini, potato, shallot, carrot and tomatoes in a large pan. Add the vegetable stock and season with salt and pepper. Bring to a boil, then cover and simmer for 20 minutes.

2 Add the green beans, peas and pasta. Cook for another 10 minutes, until the pasta is tender. Adjust the seasoning.

3 Ladle the soup into individual bowls. Combine the pesto and sun-dried tomato paste and stir a spoonful into each serving. Serve with grated Parmesan cheese to sprinkle into each bowl.

AVGOLEMONO

This is the most popular of Greek soups. The name means egg and lemon, the two important ingredients, which produce a light, nourishing soup. Orzo is a Greek pasta shaped like rice, but you can use any small shape.

7½ cups flavorful chicken stock
½ cup orzo pasta
3 eggs
juice of 1 large lemon
salt and ground black pepper
lemon slices, to garnish

SERVES 4–6

1 Pour the stock into a large pan and bring to a boil. Add the pasta and cook for 5 minutes.

2 Beat the eggs until frothy, then add the lemon juice and a tablespoon of cold water. Slowly stir in a ladleful of the hot chicken stock, then add one or two more. Return this mixture to the pan, off the heat, and stir well. Season with salt and pepper and serve immediately, garnished with lemon slices. (Do not let the soup boil once the eggs have been added or it will curdle.)

GALICIAN BROTH

This delicious main-dish soup is very similar to the warming, chunky meat and potato broths of cooler climates. For extra color, a few onion skins can be added when cooking the smoked ham, but remember to remove them before serving.

1 pound smoked ham, in one piece
2 bay leaves
2 onions, sliced
2 teaspoons paprika
1½ pounds potatoes, cut into
large chunks
½ pound collard greens
15-ounce can navy beans, drained
salt and ground black pepper

SERVES 4

2 Bring to a boil, then reduce the heat and simmer very gently for about 1½ hours, until the meat is tender. Keep an eye on the pan to make sure it doesn't boil over.

4 Cut away the cores from the greens. Roll up the leaves and cut into thin shreds. Add to the pan with the beans and simmer for about 10 minutes. Season with salt and pepper to taste and serve hot.

1 Soak the smoked ham overnight in cold water. Drain and put in a large saucepan with the bay leaves and sliced onions. Pour in 6¼ cups cold water.

3 Drain the meat, reserving the cooking liquid, and let cool slightly. Discard the skin and any excess fat from the meat and cut into small chunks. Return to the pan with the paprika and potatoes. Cover and simmer gently for 20 minutes.

COOK'S TIP
Ham hocks can be used instead of the smoked ham. The bones will give the juices a delicious flavor.

FRESH TOMATO SOUP

Intensely flavored sun-ripened tomatoes need little embellishment in this fresh-tasting soup. If you buy from the supermarket, choose the ripest-looking ones and add the amount of sugar and vinegar necessary, depending on their natural sweetness. On a hot day, this Italian soup is also delicious chilled.

3–3½ pounds ripe tomatoes
1⅔ cups flavorful chicken or
vegetable stock
3 tablespoons sun-dried tomato paste
2–3 tablespoons balsamic vinegar
2–3 teaspoons sugar
small handful basil leaves
salt and ground black pepper
basil leaves, to garnish
toasted cheese croutons and
sour cream, to serve

SERVES 6

1 Plunge the tomatoes into boiling water for 30 seconds, then refresh in cold water. Peel away the skins and quarter the tomatoes. Put them in a large saucepan and pour in the chicken or vegetable stock. Bring just to a boil, reduce the heat, cover and simmer gently for 10 minutes, until the tomatoes are soft.

2 Stir in the tomato paste, vinegar, sugar and basil. Season with salt and pepper, then cook gently, stirring, for 2 minutes. Process the soup in a blender or food processor, then return to the pan and reheat gently. Serve in bowls topped with one or two toasted cheese croutons and a spoonful of sour cream, garnished with basil leaves.

CHILLED TOMATO AND SWEET PEPPER SOUP

A recipe inspired by the Spanish gazpacho, the difference being that this soup is cooked first, and then chilled.

2 red bell peppers, halved, cored
and seeded
3 tablespoons olive oil
1 onion, finely chopped
2 garlic cloves, crushed
1½ pounds ripe tomatoes
⅔ cup red wine
2½ cups chicken stock
salt and ground black pepper
snipped fresh chives, to garnish

FOR THE CROUTONS
2 slices white bread, crusts removed
4 tablespoons olive oil

SERVES 4

1 Cut each pepper half into quarters. Place skin side up on a broiler rack and cook until the skins have charred. Transfer to a bowl and cover with a plate.

2 Heat the oil in a large pan. Add the onion and garlic and cook until soft. Meanwhile, remove the skin from the peppers and coarsely chop them. Cut the tomatoes into chunks.

3 Add the peppers and tomatoes to the pan, then cover and cook gently for 10 minutes. Add the wine and cook for another 5 minutes, then add the stock and salt and pepper and continue to simmer for 20 minutes.

4 To make the croutons, cut the bread into cubes. Heat the oil in a small frying pan, add the bread and sauté until golden. Drain on paper towels and store in an airtight box.

5 Process the soup in a blender or food processor until smooth. Pour into a clean glass or ceramic bowl and let cool thoroughly before chilling in the refrigerator for at least 3 hours. When the soup is cold, season to taste.

6 Serve the soup in bowls, topped with the croutons and garnished with snipped chives.

SPANISH GARLIC SOUP

This is a simple and satisfying soup, made with one of the most popular ingredients in the Mediterranean—garlic!

2 tablespoons olive oil
4 large garlic cloves, peeled
4 slices French bread, ¼ inch thick
1 tablespoon paprika
4 cups beef stock
¼ teaspoon ground cumin
pinch of saffron strands
4 eggs
salt and ground black pepper
chopped fresh parsley, to garnish

SERVES 4

1 Preheat the oven to 450°F. Heat the oil in a large pan. Add the whole garlic cloves and cook for a minute or two, until golden. Remove and set aside. Sauté the bread in the oil until golden, then set aside.

2 Add the paprika to the pan and sauté for a few seconds. Stir in the beef stock, cumin and saffron, then add the reserved garlic, crushing the cloves with the back of a wooden spoon. Season with salt and pepper, then cook for about 5 minutes.

3 Ladle the soup into four ovenproof bowls and break an egg into each. Set a slice of bread on top of each egg and place in the oven for 3–4 minutes, until the eggs are set. Sprinkle with parsley and serve immediately.

61

VEGETABLES

*Mediterranean vegetables are a veritable
treasure trove of taste and color that beg to be
transformed into delectable dishes.*

A Mediterranean street market is a fascinating vision of color and photo opportunities. The wonderful array of fruit and vegetable stalls in particular gives many vacationers the urge to swap their hotel rooms for a kitchen in which to cook a feast of sweet, juicy local produce. Mediterranean vegetables have an inviting irregularity about them. Uneven colorings, bumpy skins and asymmetrical shapes are a sure indication that the flesh inside will be full of flavor, a far cry from the mass-produced, artificially grown produce of colder climes. The dishes cooked using them are a joy to eat, and even the simplest tossed salad of tomatoes and greens, sprin-kled with olive oil and seasoning, is worthy of serving solo—a meal in itself.

All around the Mediterranean, vegetables are the basis of everyday meals. This is due both to the expense of meat and to the religious obligations of fasting before the many festive occasions each year. This austerity has led to the development of many imaginative cooking skills. Deep-fried, roasted, baked, stuffed, marinated, broiled, steamed, added to pies, tarts, omelets, stews and stuffings: Vegetables are very versatile.

BELOW: At a finca—or farm—in Andalusia, vegetables grow alongside the grape-drying beds.

RIGHT: Tomatoes, chiles, potatoes and braids of garlic are just some of the vegetables on sale at this market in southern Turkey.

BELOW: A golden harvest: Pumpkins make delicious soups, pies and casseroles.

In France and Italy, vegetable fritters of zucchini or eggplant, deep-fried in a light crisp batter, make a very enjoyable dish, often served with a ripe tomato sauce or garlicky herb dressing. Even the zucchini flowers are battered and fried, making a visual and interesting garnish. Ratatouille, a wonderful stew of lightly cooked vegetables, is traditionally French, although similar recipes stretch across the Mediterranean.

No vegetable is considered too small to bother with; the smallest artichokes, turnips, eggplant and fava beans are put to good use in many dishes.

A stunning variety of mushrooms appears frequently in Italian and French cooking. In these countries, markets are filled with wild varieties in the spring and autumn. The lovely shapes and flavors make interesting risottos and salads and may even be used to flavor pasta. Many mushroom varieties are dried for year-round availability. A small quantity goes a long way and can be used to liven up the flavor of everyday button mushrooms.

Stuffed vegetables are greatly loved in many countries of the Mediterranean, particularly in Turkey, Greece and the Middle East. Tomatoes, eggplant, peppers, zucchini and onions are filled with couscous, rice, herbs, spices, dried fruits, nuts, cheese and sometimes meat. Large leaves like spinach, grape and cabbage are stuffed with interesting ingredients, packed in a pan and gently cooked so as to mingle all the flavors together.

Even the humble potato takes pride of place at the Mediterranean table. The Spanish make a delicious potato salad in which new potatoes are fried to give a crisp crust. Italian gnocchi is a distinctively shaped, puréed and poached potato dish flavored with a variety of herbs, cheese or mild spices.

MARINATED MUSHROOMS

This Spanish recipe makes a nice change from the classic French mushrooms à la Grecque. Make this dish the day before you eat it; the flavor will improve with keeping.

2 tablespoons olive oil
1 small onion, very finely chopped
1 garlic clove, crushed
1 tablespoon tomato paste
¼ cup dry white wine
2 cloves
pinch of saffron strands
½ pound button mushrooms, trimmed
salt and ground black pepper
chopped fresh parsley, to garnish

SERVES 4

1 Heat the oil in a pan. Add the onion and garlic and cook until soft. Stir in the tomato paste, wine, ¼ cup water, cloves and saffron and season with salt and pepper. Bring to a boil, cover and simmer gently for about 45 minutes, adding more water if the mixture becomes too dry.

2 Add the mushrooms to the pan, then cover and simmer for another 5 minutes. Remove from the heat and, still covered, let cool. Chill overnight. Serve cold, sprinkled with chopped parsley.

POTATO AND ONION TORTILLA

One of the signature dishes of Spain, this delicious, thick potato and onion omelet is eaten at all times of the day, hot or cold.

1¼ cups olive oil
6 large potatoes, peeled and sliced
2 Spanish onions, sliced
6 eggs
salt and ground black pepper
cherry tomatoes, halved, to serve

SERVES 4

1 Heat the oil in a large nonstick frying pan. Stir in the potato, onion and a little salt. Cover and cook gently for 20 minutes, until soft.

2 Beat the eggs in a large bowl. Remove the onion and potato from the pan with a slotted spoon and add to the eggs. Season with salt and pepper to taste. Pour off some of the oil, leaving about 4 tablespoons in the pan. (Reserve the leftover oil for other cooking.) Heat the pan again.

3 When the oil is very hot, pour in the egg mixture. Cook for 2–3 minutes. Cover the pan with a plate and invert the omelet onto it. Slide it back into the pan and cook for 5 more minutes, until golden brown and moist in the middle. Serve in wedges, with the tomatoes.

BROILED EGGPLANT PARCELS

These are delicious little Italian bundles of tomatoes, mozzarella cheese and basil, wrapped in slices of eggplant.

2 large, long eggplant
8 ounces mozzarella cheese
2 plum tomatoes
16 large basil leaves
salt and ground black pepper
2 tablespoons olive oil

FOR THE DRESSING
¼ cup olive oil
1 teaspoon balsamic vinegar
1 tablespoon sun-dried tomato paste
1 tablespoon lemon juice

FOR THE GARNISH
2 tablespoons toasted pine nuts
torn basil leaves

SERVES 4

1 Remove the stems from the eggplant and cut the eggplant lengthwise into thin slices— the aim is to have a total of 16 slices, disregarding the first and last slices (each about ¼ inch thick). (If you have a mandoline, it will cut perfect, even slices for you; otherwise use a sharp, long-bladed knife.)

2 Bring a large pan of salted water to a boil and cook the eggplant slices for about 2 minutes, until just softened. Drain the sliced eggplant, then dry on paper towels.

3 Cut the mozzarella cheese into eight slices. Cut each tomato into eight slices, not counting the first and last slices.

4 Take two eggplant slices and place on an ovenproof baking sheet or dish in a cross. Place a slice of tomato in the center, season with salt and pepper, then add a basil leaf, followed by a slice of mozzarella, another basil leaf, a slice of tomato and more seasoning.

5 Fold the ends of the eggplant slices around the mozzarella and tomato filling to make a neat parcel (*left*). Repeat with the rest of the assembled ingredients to make eight parcels. Chill the parcels for about 20 minutes.

6 To make the tomato dressing, whisk together the olive oil, vinegar, sun-dried tomato paste and lemon juice. Season to taste.

7 Preheat the broiler. Brush the parcels with olive oil and cook for about 5 minutes on each side, until golden. Serve hot, with the dressing, sprinkled with pine nuts and basil.

SPINACH AND RICOTTA GNOCCHI

The success of this Italian dish lies in not overworking the mixture, to achieve delicious, light mouthfuls.

2 pounds fresh spinach
1½ cups ricotta cheese
¼ cup freshly grated
Parmesan cheese, plus extra to serve
3 eggs, beaten
¼ teaspoon grated nutmeg
3– 4 tablespoons flour
8 tablespoons butter, melted
salt and ground black pepper

SERVES 4

1. Place the spinach in a large pan and cook for 5 minutes, until wilted. Let cool, then squeeze the spinach as dry as possible. Process in a blender or food processor, then transfer to a bowl.

2. Add the ricotta, Parmesan, eggs and nutmeg. Season with salt and pepper and combine. Add enough flour to make the mixture into a soft dough. Using your hands, shape the mixture into 3-inch sausages, then dust lightly with flour.

3. Bring a large pan of salted water to a boil. Gently slide the gnocchi into the water and cook for 1–2 minutes, until they float to the surface. Remove the gnocchi with a slotted spoon and transfer to a warmed dish. Pour the melted butter over them and sprinkle with Parmesan cheese. Serve immediately.

POTATO CAKES

Delicious little fried morsels of potato and Greek feta cheese, flavored with dill and lemon juice.

1¼ pounds potatoes
4 ounces feta cheese
4 scallions, chopped
3 tablespoons chopped fresh dill
1 egg, beaten
1 tablespoon lemon juice
salt and ground black pepper
flour for dredging
3 tablespoons olive oil

SERVES 4

1 Boil the potatoes in their skins in lightly salted water until soft. Drain, then peel while still warm. Place in a bowl and mash. Crumble the feta cheese into the potatoes and add the scallions, dill, egg and lemon juice and season with salt and pepper. (The cheese is salty, so taste before you add salt.) Stir well.

2 Cover the mixture and chill until firm. Divide the mixture into walnut-size balls, then flatten them slightly. Dredge with flour. Heat the oil in a frying pan and fry the cakes until golden brown on each side. Drain on paper towels and serve immediately.

STUFFED TOMATOES AND PEPPERS

Colorful bell peppers and tomatoes make perfect containers for various meat and vegetable stuffings.
This rice and herb version uses typically Greek ingredients.

VARIATION

Small eggplant or large zucchini also make good vegetables for stuffing. Halve and scoop out the centers of the vegetables, then oil the vegetable shells and bake for about 15 minutes. Chop the centers, sauté for 2–3 minutes to soften and add to the stuffing mixture. Fill the eggplant or zucchini shells with the stuffing and bake as for the peppers and tomatoes.

2 large ripe tomatoes
1 green bell pepper
1 yellow or orange bell pepper
4 tablespoons olive oil, plus extra
for sprinkling
2 onions, chopped
2 garlic cloves, crushed
½ cup blanched almonds, chopped
scant ½ cup long-grain rice, cooked
and drained
½ ounce mint, roughly chopped
½ ounce parsley, coarsely chopped
2 tablespoons golden raisins
3 tablespoons ground almonds
salt and ground black pepper
chopped mixed herbs, to garnish

SERVES 4

1 Preheat the oven to 375°F. Cut the tomatoes in half and scoop out the pulp and seeds using a teaspoon. Leave the tomatoes to drain on paper towels with cut sides down. Coarsely chop the tomato pulp and seeds and set aside.

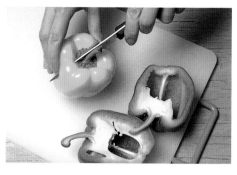

2 Halve the peppers, leaving the cores intact. Scoop out the seeds. Brush the peppers with 1 tablespoon of the oil and bake on a baking sheet for 15 minutes. Place the peppers and tomatoes in a shallow ovenproof dish and season with salt and pepper.

3 Sauté the onions in the remaining oil for 5 minutes. Add the garlic and chopped almonds and sauté for another minute.

4 Remove the pan from the heat and stir in the rice, chopped tomatoes, mint, parsley and golden raisins. Season well with salt and pepper and spoon the mixture into the tomatoes and peppers.

5 Pour ⅔ cup boiling water around the tomatoes and peppers and bake, uncovered, for 20 minutes. Scatter the ground almonds over them and sprinkle with a little extra olive oil. Return to the oven and bake for 20 more minutes, or until turning golden. Serve garnished with fresh herbs.

OKRA WITH CORIANDER AND TOMATOES

Okra is frequently combined with tomatoes and mild spices in various parts of the Mediterranean. Buy okra only if it is soft and velvety, not dry and shriveled.

*1 pound tomatoes or 14-ounce can
chopped tomatoes
1 pound fresh okra
3 tablespoons olive oil
2 onions, thinly sliced
2 teaspoons coriander seeds, crushed
3 garlic cloves, crushed
½ teaspoon sugar
finely grated zest and juice
of 1 lemon
salt and ground black pepper*

SERVES 4

1 If using fresh tomatoes, plunge them into boiling water for 30 seconds, then refresh in cold water. Peel off the skins and chop.

2 Trim off any stalks from the okra and keep whole. Heat the oil in a sauté pan and sauté the onions and coriander for 3–4 minutes, until beginning to color.

3 Add the okra and garlic and sauté for 1 minute. Gently stir in the tomatoes and sugar and simmer gently for about 20 minutes, until the okra is tender, stirring once or twice. Stir in the lemon zest and juice and add salt and pepper to taste, adding a little more sugar if necessary. Serve warm or cold.

STUFFED PEPPERS

Couscous is a form of pasta used extensively in the Middle East. It makes a good basis for a stuffing, combined with other ingredients.

6 red bell peppers
2 tablespoons butter
1 onion, finely chopped
1 teaspoon olive oil
½ teaspoon salt
1 cup instant couscous
2 tablespoons raisins
2 tablespoons chopped fresh mint
1 egg yolk
salt and ground black pepper
mint leaves, to garnish

SERVES 4

1 Preheat the oven to 400°F. Carefully slit each pepper and remove the core and seeds. Melt the butter in a small pan and add the onion. Cook until soft.

2 To cook the couscous, bring 1 cup water to a boil. Add the olive oil and the salt, then remove the pan from the heat and add the couscous. Stir and let stand, covered, for about 5 minutes. Stir in the cooked onion, raisins and mint, then season well with salt and pepper. Stir in the egg yolk.

3 Using a teaspoon, fill the peppers with the couscous mixture to only about three-quarters full, as the couscous will swell when cooked further. Place in a lightly oiled ovenproof dish and bake, uncovered, for about 20 minutes, until tender. Serve hot or cold, garnished with the mint leaves.

VEGETABLES

ZUCCHINI FRITTERS WITH PISTOU

These delicious fritters are a specialty of southern France. The pistou sauce provides a lovely contrast in flavor, but you could substitute other sauces, like a garlicky tomato sauce or an herb dressing.

FOR THE PISTOU
½ ounce basil leaves
4 garlic cloves, crushed
1 cup grated Parmesan cheese
finely grated zest of 1 lemon
⅔ cup olive oil

FOR THE FRITTERS
1 pound zucchini, grated
⅔ cup flour
1 egg, separated
1 tablespoon olive oil
oil for shallow-frying
salt and ground black pepper

SERVES 4

1 To make the pistou, crush the basil leaves and garlic with a mortar and pestle to make a fairly fine paste. Transfer the paste to a bowl and stir in the grated cheese and lemon zest. Gradually blend in the oil, a little at a time, until combined, then transfer to a small serving dish.

2 To make the fritters, put the grated zucchini in a strainer over a bowl and sprinkle with plenty of salt. Let sit for 1 hour, then rinse thoroughly. Dry well on paper towels.

3 Sift the flour into a bowl and make a well in the center, then add the egg yolk and oil. Measure 5 tablespoons water and add a little to the bowl.

4 Beat the egg yolk and oil, gradually incorporating the flour and water to make a smooth batter. Season and let sit for 30 minutes.

5 Stir the zucchini into the batter. Beat the egg white until stiff, then fold into the batter.

6 Heat ½ inch of oil in a frying pan. Add spoonfuls of batter to the oil and fry for 2 minutes, until golden. Drain the fritters on paper towels and keep warm while frying the rest. Serve with the sauce.

RATATOUILLE

A highly versatile vegetable stew from Provence, ratatouille is delicious hot or cold, on its own or with eggs, pasta, fish or meat—particularly roast lamb.

2 pounds ripe tomatoes
½ cup olive oil
2 onions, thinly sliced
2 red bell peppers, seeded and cut into chunks
1 yellow or orange bell pepper, seeded and cut into chunks
1 large eggplant, cut into chunks
2 zucchini, cut into thick slices
4 garlic cloves, crushed
2 bay leaves
1 tablespoon chopped young thyme
salt and ground black pepper

SERVES 6

 Plunge the tomatoes into boiling water for 30 seconds, then refresh in cold water. Peel and chop coarsely.

Heat a little of the oil in a large, heavy pan and sauté the onions for 5 minutes. Add the peppers and sauté for another 2 minutes. Drain. Add the eggplant and more oil and sauté gently for 5 minutes. Add the remaining oil and zucchini and sauté for 3 minutes. Drain.

Add the garlic and tomatoes to the pan with the bay leaves and thyme and a little salt and pepper. Cook gently until the tomatoes have softened and are turning pulpy.

 Return all the vegetables to the pan and cook gently, stirring frequently, for about 15 minutes, until fairly pulpy but retaining a little texture. Season with more salt and pepper to taste.

COOK'S TIP
There are no specific quantities for the vegetables when making ratatouille, so you can, to a large extent, vary the quantities and types of vegetables depending on what you have in the refrigerator. If the tomatoes are a little tasteless, add 2–3 tablespoons tomato paste and a dash of sugar to the mixture along with the tomatoes.

SPINACH WITH RAISINS AND PINE NUTS

Raisins and pine nuts are frequent partners in Spanish recipes. Here, tossed with wilted spinach and croutons, they make a delicious snack or main-dish accompaniment.

⅓ cup raisins
1 thick slice crusty white bread
3 tablespoons olive oil
⅓ cup pine nuts
1¼ pounds young spinach,
stems removed
2 garlic cloves, crushed
salt and ground black pepper

SERVES 4

1 Put the raisins in a small bowl with boiling water and let soak for 10 minutes. Drain.

2 Cut the bread into cubes and discard the crusts. Heat 2 tablespoons of the oil and fry the bread until golden. Drain.

3 Heat the remaining oil in the pan. Sauté the pine nuts until beginning to color. Add the spinach and garlic and cook quickly, turning the spinach until it has just wilted.

4 Toss in the raisins and season lightly with salt and pepper. Transfer to a warmed serving dish. Sprinkle croutons on top and serve hot.

VARIATION
Use Swiss chard or beet greens instead of the spinach, cooking them a little longer.

SPICED TURNIPS WITH SPINACH AND TOMATOES

Sweet baby turnips, tender spinach and ripe tomatoes make tempting partners in this simple eastern Mediterranean vegetable stew.

1 pound plum or other
ripe tomatoes
¼ cup olive oil
2 onions, sliced
1 pound baby turnips, peeled
1 teaspoon paprika
½ teaspoon sugar
4 tablespoons chopped cilantro
1 pound fresh young spinach,
stalks removed
salt and ground black pepper

SERVES 6

1 Plunge the tomatoes into a bowl of boiling water for 30 seconds, then refresh in a bowl of cold water. Peel away the tomato skins and chop coarsely. Heat the olive oil in a large frying pan or sauté pan and sauté the onion slices for about 5 minutes until golden.

2 Add the baby turnips, tomatoes and paprika to the pan with ¼ cup water and cook until the tomatoes are pulpy. Cover with a lid and continue cooking until the baby turnips have softened.

3 Stir in the sugar and cilantro, then add the spinach and a little salt and pepper and cook for another 2–3 minutes, until the spinach has wilted. Serve warm or cold.

STUFFED GRAPE LEAVES WITH GARLIC YOGURT

An old Greek recipe that comes in many guises. This meatless version is highly flavored with fresh herbs, lemon and a little chile.

8 ounces preserved grape leaves
1 onion, finely chopped
½ bunch of scallions, trimmed and
finely chopped
¼ cup chopped fresh parsley
10 large mint sprigs, chopped
finely grated zest of 1 lemon
½ teaspoon crushed dried chiles
1½ teaspoons fennel seeds, crushed
scant 1 cup long-grain rice
½ cup olive oil
⅔ cup thick plain yogurt
2 garlic cloves, crushed
salt
lemon wedges and mint leaves,
to garnish (optional)

SERVES 6

1 Rinse the grape leaves in plenty of cold water. Put in a bowl, cover with boiling water and let sit for 10 minutes. Drain thoroughly.

2 Combine the onion, scallions, parsley, mint, lemon, chiles, fennel, rice and 1½ tablespoons of the olive oil. Mix thoroughly and season with salt.

3 Place a grape leaf, veined side facing upward, on a work surface and cut off any stem. Place a heaping teaspoonful of the rice mixture near the stem end of the leaf.

4 Fold the stem end of the leaf over the rice filling, then fold over the sides and carefully roll up into a neat cigar shape.

5 Repeat with the remaining filling to make about 28 stuffed leaves. If some of the grape leaves are quite small, use two and patch them together to make parcels of the same size as the others.

6 Place any remaining leaves in the bottom of a large, heavy saucepan. Pack the stuffed leaves in a single layer in the pan. Spoon on the remaining oil, then add about 1¼ cups boiling water.

COOK'S TIP
To check that the rice is cooked, lift out one stuffed leaf and cut in half. The rice should have expanded and softened to make a firm parcel. If necessary, cook the stuffed leaves a little longer, adding boiling water if the pan is becoming dry.

7 Place a small plate over the leaves to keep them submerged in the water. Cover the pan and cook over very low heat for 45 minutes.

8 Combine the yogurt and garlic and place in a small serving dish. Transfer the stuffed leaves to a serving plate and garnish with lemon wedges and mint, if desired. Serve with the garlic yogurt.

SPICY CHICKPEA AND EGGPLANT STEW

This is a Lebanese dish, but similar dishes are found all over the Mediterranean.

3 large eggplant, cubed
1 cup chickpeas, soaked overnight
¼ cup olive oil
3 garlic cloves, chopped
2 large onions, chopped
½ teaspoon ground cumin
½ teaspoon ground cinnamon
2½ teaspoons ground coriander
3 14-ounce cans chopped tomatoes
salt and ground black pepper
cooked rice, to serve

FOR THE GARNISH
2 tablespoons olive oil
1 onion, sliced
1 garlic clove, sliced
sprigs of cilantro

SERVES 4

1 Place the eggplant pieces in a colander and sprinkle them with salt. Set the colander in a bowl and let sit for 30 minutes, to allow the bitter juices to escape. Rinse with cold water and dry on paper towels.

2 Drain the chickpeas and put in a pan with enough water to cover. Bring to a boil and simmer for 30 minutes or until tender. Drain.

3 Heat the oil in a large pan. Add the garlic and onions and cook gently, until soft. Add the spices and cook, stirring, for a few seconds. Add the eggplant and stir to coat with the spices and onion. Cook for 5 minutes. Add the tomatoes and chickpeas and season with salt and pepper. Cover and simmer for 20 minutes.

4 To make the garnish, heat the oil in a frying pan and, when very hot, add the sliced onion and garlic. Fry until golden and crisp. Serve the stew with rice, topped with the onion and garlic and garnished with cilantro.

SPANISH POTATOES

This is an adaptation of a peppery potato dish of which there are several versions. All of them are fried and mildly spiced with the added tang of wine vinegar. Serve with cold meats or as a tapa.

1½ pounds small new potatoes
5 tablespoons olive oil
2 garlic cloves, sliced
½ teaspoon crushed dried chiles
½ teaspoon ground cumin
2 teaspoons paprika
2 tablespoons red or white
wine vinegar
1 red or green bell pepper, seeded
and sliced
coarse sea salt, to serve (optional)

SERVES 4

1 Cook the potatoes in boiling salted water until almost tender. Drain and, if preferred, peel them. Cut into chunks.

2 Heat the oil in a large frying or sauté pan and fry the potatoes, turning them frequently, until golden.

3 Meanwhile, crush together the garlic, chiles and cumin using a mortar and pestle. Mix with the paprika and wine vinegar.

4 Add the garlic mixture to the potatoes with the sliced pepper and cook, stirring, for 2 minutes. Serve warm, or let sit until cold. Sprinkle with coarse sea salt, if desired, to serve.

SALADS

❦❦

*Summer and salads are synonymous, and
nowhere is there a wider variety of these flavorful
dishes than in the Mediterranean.*

LEFT: Some of these plump Moroccan olives will find their way into salads, but the majority will be pressed for oil.

oil, and seasoned with salt and pepper. There are many variations, using different ingredients such as lemon juice, mustard, herbs, garlic and cream; the types of oils and vinegars can be varied too. Extra virgin olive oil gives the finest flavor of all the olive oils, but a mixture of peanut oil and olive oil will produce a lighter dressing. Nut oils, such as walnut, complement salads containing nuts. The Italians favor a good red wine vinegar, but there is also the sour/sweet flavor of balsamic vinegar to consider—delicious with broiled vegetables. Spanish sherry vinegar is another good flavor to try. Herb-infused vinegars are also useful, particularly if the fresh herbs are unavailable.

There is an abundant variety of salad greens in the Mediterranean, ranging in color, taste and texture. The French favor a mixture of leaves called mesclun, which can be bought at markets by the handful. Dandelion greens are popular too, as well as frisée, Belgian endive, red leaf lettuce and many more. In Italy, radicchio and arugula are preferred, and the Spanish favor romaine lettuce. In

The climate of the Mediterranean countries has ensured that salads and cold dishes have always been popular. There is an abundance of wonderful ingredients, particularly vegetables, which are combined to produce delicious results. In its simplest form, a salad in France, Spain or Italy would consist of lettuce, or perhaps a mixture of a few different salad greens, dressed with vinaigrette. A salad may be eaten after the main course, often before the cheese is served. Vinaigrette is the basic salad dressing. Originally a French classic, it is now used worldwide. As its name suggests, vinegar is a main ingredient, combined with three times its quantity of olive

RIGHT: Visiting a Turkish market is more than a mere shopping trip; it's a chance to catch up on local news.

ABOVE: A quiet landscape near Carmona in the beautiful region of Andalusia in southern Spain.

the Middle East, however, green salads are less popular. Salads of cooked or raw vegetables, dressed with a lemony vinaigrette, are more typical of these countries. Fresh herbs also play an important part, sometimes served alone, between courses, to cleanse the palate. These basic salads are spontaneous, depending on what is available in the market, and need no recipes.

The markets of the Mediterranean offer some of the best vegetables and fruit in the world. From huge vine-ripened tomatoes to tiny artichokes, all are lovingly displayed, waiting to be picked up and dropped into a basket to be taken home. The inspiration for salads is endless. Fruit too, is included; grapes and oranges make refreshing additions to some of our recipes.

Apart from the simple salads, there are the composed salads—specific ingredients, with a special dressing, which are dishes on their own, to be eaten as a lunch dish, or perhaps an appetizer. These salads include all sorts of foods: olives, sausage, nuts, cheese, anchovies—morsels chosen for a contrast in taste, texture and color.

This chapter includes some of the classic salads of the region, including Salad Niçoise and Greek Salad, both of which are sure to transport anyone who has eaten them in their native countries straight to a little village on the coast of the Mediterranean. Some salads are substantial enough to be served as a main dish, such as Roasted Peppers with Tomatoes and Anchovies or Fava Bean, Mushroom and Chorizo Salad. Bread and a glass of wine should complete the picture!

ROASTED PEPPERS WITH TOMATOES AND ANCHOVIES

This is a Sicilian-style salad, using some typical ingredients from the Italian island. The flavor improves if the salad is made and dressed an hour or two before serving.

1 red bell pepper
1 yellow bell pepper
4 sun-dried tomatoes in oil, drained
4 ripe plum tomatoes, sliced
2 canned anchovies, drained
and chopped
1 tablespoon capers, drained
1 tablespoon pine nuts
1 garlic clove, very thinly sliced

FOR THE DRESSING
5 tablespoons extra virgin olive oil
1 tablespoon balsamic vinegar
1 teaspoon lemon juice
chopped fresh mixed herbs
salt and ground black pepper

SERVES 4

1 Cut the peppers in half and remove the seeds and stems. Cut into quarters and cook, skin side up, under a hot broiler, until the skin chars. Transfer to a bowl and cover with a plate. Let cool. Peel the peppers and cut into strips.

2 Thinly slice the sun-dried tomatoes. Arrange the peppers and fresh tomatoes on a serving dish. Sprinkle the anchovies, sun-dried tomatoes, capers, pine nuts and garlic on top.

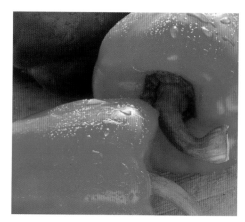

3 To make the dressing, combine the olive oil, vinegar, lemon juice and chopped herbs and season with salt and pepper. Pour over the salad just before serving.

SWEET-AND-SOUR ONION SALAD

This recipe is primarily from Provence in the south of France, but there are influences from other Mediterranean countries, too.

1 pound baby onions, peeled
¼ cup wine vinegar
3 tablespoons olive oil
3 tablespoons sugar
3 tablespoons tomato paste
1 bay leaf
2 parsley sprigs
½ cup raisins
salt and ground black pepper

SERVES 6

1 Put all the ingredients in a pan with 1¼ cups water. Bring to a boil and simmer gently, uncovered, for 45 minutes or until the onions are tender and most of the liquid has evaporated.

2 Remove the bay leaf and parsley, check the seasoning and transfer to a serving dish. Serve at room temperature.

GREEK SALAD

Anyone who has spent a vacation in Greece will have eaten a version of this salad—the Greek equivalent of a mixed salad. Its success relies on using the freshest of ingredients and a good olive oil.

1 small head romaine lettuce, sliced
1 pound ripe tomatoes, cut into eighths
1 cucumber, seeded and chopped
7 ounces feta cheese, crumbled
4 scallions, sliced
½ cup black olives, pitted and halved

FOR THE DRESSING
6 tablespoons good olive oil
1½ tablespoons lemon juice
salt and ground black pepper

SERVES 6

 Put all the main salad ingredients into a large bowl. Whisk together the olive oil and lemon juice, then season with salt and pepper, and pour the dressing on the salad. Mix well and serve immediately.

SPICED EGGPLANT SALAD

Serve this Middle Eastern-influenced salad with warm pita bread as an appetizer or to accompany a main-course rice pilaf.

2 small eggplant, sliced
5 tablespoons olive oil
¼ cup red wine vinegar
2 garlic cloves, crushed
1 tablespoon lemon juice
½ teaspoon ground cumin
½ teaspoon ground coriander
½ cucumber, thinly sliced
2 ripe tomatoes, thinly sliced
2 tablespoons plain yogurt
salt and ground black pepper
chopped flat-leaf parsley, to garnish

SERVES 4

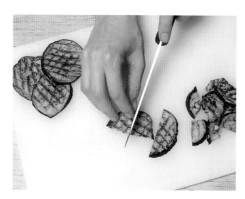

 Preheat the broiler. Brush the eggplant slices lightly with some of the oil and cook under high heat, turning once, until golden and tender. Cut into quarters.

2 Combine the remaining oil, vinegar, garlic, lemon juice, cumin and coriander. Season with salt and pepper and mix thoroughly. Add the warm eggplant, stir well and chill for at least 2 hours. Add the cucumber and tomatoes. Transfer to a serving dish and spoon the yogurt on top. Sprinkle with parsley.

PANZANELLA

In this lively Italian specialty, a sweet, tangy blend of tomato juice, rich olive oil and red wine vinegar is soaked up in a colorful salad of roasted peppers, anchovies and toasted ciabatta.

8 ounces ciabatta (about ⅔ loaf)
⅔ cup olive oil
3 red bell peppers
3 yellow bell peppers
2-ounce can anchovy fillets
1½ pounds ripe plum tomatoes
4 garlic cloves, crushed
4 tablespoons red wine vinegar
¼ cup caperberries or capers
1 cup pitted black olives
salt and ground black pepper
basil leaves, to garnish

SERVES 4–6

1. Preheat the oven to 400°F. Cut the ciabatta into ¾-inch chunks and drizzle with ¼ cup of the olive oil. Bake lightly until a pale golden color.

2. Put the peppers on a foil-lined baking sheet and bake for about 45 minutes, until the skin begins to char. Remove from the oven, cover with a cloth and let cool slightly.

3. Pull the skin off the peppers and cut them into quarters, discarding the stem ends and seeds. Drain and then coarsely chop the anchovies. Set aside.

4. To make the tomato dressing, peel and halve the tomatoes. Scoop the seeds into a strainer set over a bowl. Using the back of a spoon, press the tomato pulp in the strainer to extract as much juice as possible. Discard the pulp and add the remaining oil, the garlic and vinegar to the juices.

5. Layer the toasted bread, peppers, tomatoes, anchovies, capers and olives in a large salad bowl. Season the tomato dressing with salt and pepper and pour it over the salad. Let stand for about 30 minutes. Serve garnished with plenty of basil leaves.

RADICCHIO, ARTICHOKE AND WALNUT SALAD

The distinctive, earthy taste of Jerusalem artichokes makes a lovely contrast to the sharp freshness of radicchio and lemon. Serve warm or cold as an accompaniment to broiled steak or grilled meats.

1 large head radicchio or 5 ounces
radicchio leaves
6 tablespoons walnut pieces
3 tablespoons walnut oil
1¼ pounds Jerusalem artichokes
pared zest and juice of 1 lemon
coarse sea salt and ground
black pepper
flat-leaf parsley, to garnish (optional)

SERVES 4

1. If using a whole radicchio, cut it into 8–10 wedges. Put the wedges or leaves in a flameproof dish. Sprinkle the walnuts on top, then spoon on the oil and season. Broil for 2–3 minutes.

2. Peel the artichokes and cut up any large ones so the pieces are all roughly the same size. Add the artichokes to a pan of boiling salted water with half the lemon juice and cook for 5–7 minutes, until tender. Drain. Preheat the broiler to high.

3. Toss the artichokes into the salad with the remaining lemon juice and the pared zest. Season with coarse salt and pepper. Broil until beginning to brown. Serve immediately garnished with torn pieces of parsley, if desired.

CACIK

—

This refreshing yogurt dish is served all over the eastern Mediterranean, whether as part of a mezze with marinated olives and pita bread or as an accompaniment to meat dishes. Greek tzatziki is very similar.

1 small cucumber
1¼ cups thick plain yogurt
3 garlic cloves, crushed
2 tablespoons chopped fresh mint
2 tablespoons chopped fresh dill
or parsley
salt and ground black pepper
mint or parsley and dill, to garnish
olive oil, olives and pita bread,
to serve

SERVES 6

1 Finely chop the cucumber and layer in a colander with plenty of salt. Let sit for 30 minutes. Wash the cucumber in several changes of cold water and drain thoroughly. Pat dry on paper towels.

2 Combine the yogurt, garlic and herbs and season with salt and pepper. Stir in the cucumber. Garnish with herbs, drizzle on a little olive oil and serve with olives and pita bread.

BROWN BEAN SALAD

Brown beans, sometimes called "ful medames," are widely used in Egyptian cooking and are occasionally seen in health-food stores here. Dried fava beans or black or red kidney beans make a good substitute.

1½ cups dried brown beans
3 thyme sprigs
2 bay leaves
1 onion, halved
4 garlic cloves, crushed
1½ teaspoons cumin seeds, crushed
3 scallions, finely chopped
6 tablespoons coarsely chopped
fresh flat-leaf parsley
4 teaspoons lemon juice
6 tablespoons olive oil
3 hard-boiled eggs, shelled and
coarsely chopped
1 dill pickle, roughly chopped
salt and ground black pepper

SERVES 6

1   Put the beans in a bowl with plenty of cold water and let soak overnight. Drain, transfer to a saucepan and cover with fresh water. Bring to a boil and boil rapidly for 10 minutes.

2   Reduce the heat and add the thyme, bay leaves and onion. Simmer very gently for about 1 hour, until tender. Drain and discard the herbs and onion.

COOK'S TIP
The cooking time for dried beans can vary considerably. They may need only 45 minutes or a lot longer.

3   Combine the garlic, cumin, scallions, parsley, lemon juice, oil and add a little salt and pepper. Pour over the beans and toss the ingredients together lightly.

4   Gently stir in the eggs and pickle and serve immediately.

WARM FAVA BEAN AND FETA SALAD

This recipe is loosely based on a typical medley of fresh-tasting Greek salad ingredients—fava beans, tomatoes and feta cheese. It's great warm or cold, as an appetizer or main-course accompaniment.

2 pounds fava beans, shelled, or
12 ounces shelled frozen beans
4 tablespoons olive oil
6 ounces plum tomatoes, halved, or
quartered if large
4 garlic cloves, crushed
4 ounces firm feta cheese, cut
into chunks
3 tablespoons chopped fresh dill
12 black olives
salt and ground black pepper
chopped fresh dill, to garnish

SERVES 4–6

1 Cook the fresh or frozen fava beans in boiling salted water until just tender. Drain and set aside.

2 Meanwhile, heat the oil in a heavy frying pan and add the tomatoes and garlic. Cook until the tomatoes are beginning to color.

3 Add the feta to the pan and toss the ingredients together for 1 minute. Mix with the drained beans, dill, olives and salt and pepper. Serve garnished with chopped dill.

HALLOUMI AND GRAPE SALAD

In Eastern Europe, firm, salty halloumi cheese is often served fried for breakfast or supper. Feta cheese makes a good substitute in this recipe.

FOR THE DRESSING
¼ cup olive oil
1 tablespoon lemon juice
½ teaspoon sugar
salt and ground black pepper
1 tablespoon chopped fresh thyme
or dill

FOR THE SALAD
5 ounces mixed salad greens
3 ounces seedless green grapes
3 ounces seedless red grapes
9 ounces halloumi cheese
3 tablespoons olive oil
thyme leaves or dill, to garnish

SERVES 4

1 To make the dressing, combine the olive oil, lemon juice and sugar. Season. Stir in the thyme or dill and set aside.

2 Toss together the salad greens and the green and red grapes, then transfer to a large serving plate.

3 Thinly slice the cheese. Heat the oil in a large frying pan. Add the cheese and sauté briefly until turning golden on the underside. Turn the cheese with a spatula and cook the other side.

4 Arrange the cheese on the salad. Pour on the dressing and garnish with thyme or dill.

SALAD NIÇOISE

Made with good-quality ingredients, this Provençal salad makes a simple yet unbeatable summer lunch or supper dish. Serve with country-style bread and chilled white wine.

FOR THE DRESSING
6 tablespoons extra virgin olive oil
2 garlic cloves, crushed
1 tablespoon white wine vinegar
salt and ground black pepper

FOR THE SALAD
4 ounces green beans, trimmed
4 ounces mixed salad greens
½ small cucumber, thinly sliced
4 ripe tomatoes, quartered
7-ounce can tuna in oil, drained
2-ounce can anchovies, drained
4 eggs, hard-boiled
½ bunch radishes, trimmed
½ cup small black olives
flat-leaf parsley, to garnish

SERVES 4

1 To make the dressing, whisk together the oil, garlic and vinegar and season to taste with salt and pepper.

2 Halve the green beans and cook in a saucepan of boiling water for 2 minutes, until only just tender; drain.

3 Mix the salad greens, cucumber, tomatoes and green beans in a large, shallow salad bowl. Flake the tuna. Halve the anchovies lengthwise. Shell and quarter the eggs.

4 Sprinkle the radishes, tuna, anchovies, eggs and olives on the salad. Pour the dressing over and toss together lightly. Serve garnished with parsley.

SPANISH ASPARAGUS AND ORANGE SALAD

Complicated salad dressings are rarely found in Spain—they simply rely on the wonderful flavor of a good-quality olive oil.

8 ounces asparagus, trimmed and cut into 2-inch pieces
2 large oranges
2 ripe tomatoes, cut into eighths
2 ounces romaine lettuce leaves, shredded
2 tablespoons extra virgin olive oil
½ teaspoon sherry vinegar
salt and ground black pepper

SERVES 4

COOK'S TIP
Bibb lettuce can be used in place of romaine.

1 Cook the asparagus in boiling, salted water for 3–4 minutes, until just tender. Drain and refresh under cold water.

2 Grate the zest from half an orange and reserve. Peel all the oranges and cut into segments. Squeeze out the juice from the membrane and reserve the juice.

3 Put the asparagus, orange segments, tomatoes and lettuce into a salad bowl. Combine the oil and vinegar and add 1 tablespoon of the reserved orange juice and 1 teaspoon of the zest *(left)*. Season with salt and pepper. Just before serving, pour the dressing over the salad and mix gently to coat.

GLOBE ARTICHOKES WITH GREEN BEANS AND AIOLI

Just like the French aïoli, there are many recipes for the Spanish equivalent. This one is exceptionally garlicky, a perfect partner to freshly cooked vegetables.

FOR THE AIOLI
6 large garlic cloves, sliced
2 teaspoons white wine vinegar
1 cup olive oil
salt and ground black pepper

FOR THE SALAD
8 ounces green beans
3 small globe artichokes
1 tablespoon olive oil
pared zest of 1 lemon
coarse salt for sprinkling
lemon wedges, to garnish

SERVES 4–6

1 To make the aïoli, put the garlic and vinegar in a blender or mini food processor. With the machine switched on, gradually pour in the olive oil until the mixture is thickened and smooth. (Alternatively, crush the garlic to a paste with the vinegar and gradually beat in the oil using a hand whisk.) Season with salt and pepper to taste.

2 To make the salad, cook the beans in boiling water for 1–2 minutes, until slightly softened. Drain.

3 Trim the artichoke stems close to the base. Cook the artichokes in a large pan of salted water for about 30 minutes or until you can easily pull away a leaf from the base. Drain well.

4 Using a sharp knife, halve the artichokes lengthwise and ease out the choke using a teaspoon.

5 Arrange the artichokes and beans on serving plates and drizzle with the oil. Sprinkle on the lemon zest and season with coarse salt and a little pepper. Spoon the aïoli into the artichoke hearts and serve warm, garnished with lemon wedges. To eat artichokes, pull the leaves from the base one at a time and use to scoop a little of the sauce. It is only the fleshy end of each leaf that is eaten, as well as the base or heart of the artichoke.

COOK'S TIP
Mediterranean baby artichokes are sometimes available and are perfect for this kind of salad, as unlike the larger ones, they can be eaten whole. Cook them until just tender, then cut in half to serve.
Canned artichoke hearts, thoroughly drained and sliced, can be substituted when fresh ones are not available.

FAVA BEAN, MUSHROOM AND CHORIZO SALAD

Fava beans are used in both their fresh and dried forms in various Mediterranean countries. This Spanish salad could be served as either a first course or a lunch dish.

8 ounces shelled fava beans
6 ounces chorizo sausage
4 tablespoons extra virgin olive oil
8 ounces cremini
mushrooms, sliced
handful of fresh chives
salt and ground black pepper

SERVES 4

1   Cook the fava beans in boiling salted water for about 8 minutes. Drain and refresh under cold water.

2   Remove the skin from the sausage and cut it into small chunks. Heat the oil in a frying pan, add the chorizo and cook for 2–3 minutes. Pour the chorizo and oil into the mushrooms and mix well. Let cool. Chop half the chives. If the beans are large, peel off the tough outer skins. Stir the beans and snipped chives into the mushroom mixture and season to taste. Serve at room temperature, garnished with the remaining chives.

AVOCADO, ORANGE AND ALMOND SALAD

The Mediterranean is not particularly known for its avocados, but the climate is perfect for them and they are grown in many parts of the region. This salad has a Spanish influence.

2 oranges
2 ripe tomatoes
2 small avocados
¼ cup extra virgin olive oil
2 tablespoons lemon juice
1 tablespoon chopped fresh parsley
1 small onion, sliced into rings
salt and ground black pepper
¼ cup sliced almonds and
10–12 black olives, to garnish

SERVES 4

1   Peel the oranges and cut into thick slices. Plunge the tomatoes into boiling water for 30 seconds, then refresh in cold water. Peel off the skins, cut into quarters, remove the seeds and chop coarsely.

2   Cut the avocados in half, remove the pits and carefully peel off the skin. Cut into chunks.

3   Combine the olive oil, lemon juice and parsley. Season with salt and pepper. Toss the avocados and tomatoes in half of the dressing.

4   Arrange the sliced oranges on a plate and scatter the onion rings over them. Drizzle with the rest of the dressing. Spoon the avocados, tomatoes, almonds and olives on top.

FISH AND SHELLFISH

Mediterranean fishermen reap a rich harvest of fish and shellfish, which are often simply broiled or fried, or used as the basis of a soup or stew.

FISH AND SHELLFISH

The Mediterranean Sea is tiny in relation to the world's larger seas and oceans. It is also relatively shallow, warm, low in natural food supplies and more polluted. Despite all these factors, the Mediterranean has hundreds of different species of fish and crustacea, marketed in the Mediterranean and beyond. Visit a large fish market in any part of the region and you will be amazed by the fantastic variety of fish, many of which are completely unknown except to the locals and, of course, the fishermen themselves.

ABOVE: Fishermen in Crete bring home the day's catch, packed in salt.

LEFT: Safely back in harbor, a Cretan fishing boat bobs gently on the calm sea.

A visit to a Mediterranean restaurant, bar or taverna illustrates how this freshly caught fish, cooked simply, can be quite unbeatable. Few of us ever forget the arrival of a hot, steaming bowl of garlicky mussels or crisp shrimp dripping in garlic and olive oil. Perfectly fresh fish, broiled or grilled with a basting of olive oil, garlic and herbs, needs little more embellishment, except perhaps a crisp salad and a light wine.

On a more elaborate scale, fish stews and soups are typically Mediterranean. A varied mixture of fish such as conger eel, gurnard, John Dory, monkfish, bass, bream and red mullet is combined with aromatic flavorings like saffron, herbs, garlic and orange peel and cooked in an intensely flavored fish stock made from fish trimmings. The bourride of France and the brodetto of Italy are classic examples but similar variations can be found all over the Mediterranean.

Small, oily fish thrive in the Mediterranean, and the

108

ABOVE: A Moroccan cook patiently prepares the family meal of fish kebabs.

freshly broiled or grilled sardines prepared in cafés and tavernas around the region cannot be rivaled anywhere else in the world. Sardines and large anchovies are sometimes stuffed with a slightly tangy mixture of ingredients, such as capers, olives, pine nuts, lemons and dried fruit, that provides a perfect contrast to the rich oiliness of the fish itself. Other interesting preparations are the short-term preserving of fried sardines in olive oil and vinegar or the delicious combination of sardines with fresh herbs and spaghetti or macaroni.

The technique of frying fish in a light batter is typical of the Mediterranean. Fritto Misto is an Italian version in which a medley of seafood, such as mussels, squid, red mullet, shrimp and whitebait, is coated in a light crisp batter and deep-fried. When served piping hot, this is

delicious as a light snack or appetizer with a spinkling of gremolata (a blend of garlic, parsley and lemon zest), or simply squeezed with lemon. The Spanish also love fried fish and use much the same technique, sometimes simply dredging the fish with seasoned flour before frying in light olive oil.

Taking into consideration the availability of so much fresh produce, it is surprising that salt cod is so well loved in various parts of the Mediterranean; the kite-shaped, leathery pieces are a common sight in many marketplaces. The Spanish and Portuguese fished for cod in the Atlantic, salted it and sun-dried it at sea as a means of preservation. These familiar stiff, yellow-tinged boards of fish, which once were associated with the frugal eating of Lent, are now a highly esteemed luxury. Perhaps the most famous dish is the brandade of France, a smooth purée of salt cod flavored with garlic and olive oil.

On the eastern side of the Mediterranean the types of fish available are much the same, although the cooking methods vary. Baking fish whole is the most widespread practice, often on a bed of tomatoes, lemons, onions and herbs, and sometimes with slightly sweet and spicy flavorings such as raisins and cinnamon. The Greek plaki is a well-loved example, perfect for fish such as gray mullet, sea bream and bass, which absorb all the wonderful flavors of the accompanying ingredients. Middle Eastern and North African fish dishes emphasize the accompanying sauce—the choice of fish being the pick of the catch. A simple blend of tahini with olive oil and lemon juice is very traditional.

Squid and octopus both play an important role in Mediterranean cooking. Squid, from the tiniest, which are lovely seared in olive oil with garlic and herbs, to huge specimens, rich with stuffings, typify Mediterranean cooking techniques. Octopus, too, is highly esteemed, particularly in the eastern Mediterranean, where it is frequently stewed with red wine or used in salads.

PANFRIED RED MULLET WITH BASIL AND CITRUS

Red mullet is popular all over the Mediterranean. This Italian recipe combines it with oranges and lemons, which grow in abundance there.

4 red mullet (or snapper), about 8
ounces each, filleted
6 tablespoons olive oil
10 peppercorns, crushed
2 oranges, one peeled and sliced and
one squeezed
1 lemon
2 tablespoons flour
1 tablespoon butter
2 drained canned anchovies, chopped
4 tablespoons shredded fresh basil
salt and ground black pepper

SERVES 4

1 Place the fish fillets in a shallow dish in a single layer. Pour the olive oil over them and sprinkle with the crushed peppercorns. Lay the orange slices on top of the fish. Cover the dish and let marinate in the refrigerator for at least 4 hours.

2 Halve the lemon. Remove the zest and pith from one half using a small sharp knife and slice thinly. Squeeze the juice from the other half.

3 Lift the fish out of the marinade and pat dry on paper towels. Reserve the marinade and orange slices. Season the fish with salt and pepper and dust lightly with flour.

4 Heat 3 tablespoons of the marinade in a frying pan. Add the fish and fry for 2 minutes on each side. Remove from the pan and keep warm. Discard the marinade that is left in the pan.

5 Melt the butter in the pan with any of the remaining original marinade. Add the anchovies and cook until completely softened.

6 Stir in the orange and lemon juice, then check the seasoning and simmer until slightly reduced. Stir in the basil. Pour the sauce on the fish and garnish with the reserved orange slices and the lemon slices.

COOK'S TIP
If you prefer, use other fish fillets
for this dish, such as red snapper,
lemon sole, haddock or hake.

SEAFOOD RISOTTO

Risotto is one of Italy's most popular rice dishes, and it is made with everything from pumpkin to squid ink. On the Mediterranean shores, seafood is the most obvious addition.

¼ cup sunflower oil
1 onion, chopped
2 garlic cloves, crushed
generous 1 cup arborio rice
7 tablespoons white wine
6¼ cups hot fish stock
12 ounces mixed seafood, such as
raw shrimp, mussels, squid rings
or clams
grated zest of ½ lemon
2 tablespoons tomato paste
1 tablespoon chopped fresh parsley
salt and ground black pepper

SERVES 4

1 Heat the oil in a heavy pan, add the onion and garlic and cook until soft. Add the rice and stir to coat the grains with oil. Add the wine and cook, stirring, over medium heat, for a few minutes until absorbed.

2 Add ⅔ cup of the hot fish stock and cook, stirring constantly, until the liquid is absorbed by the rice. Continue stirring and adding stock in ⅔ cup quantities, until half of the stock is left. This should take about 10 minutes.

3 Stir in the seafood and cook for 2–3 minutes. Add the remaining stock as before, until the rice is cooked. It should be quite creamy and the grains al dente.

4 Stir in the lemon zest, tomato paste and parsley. Season with salt and pepper and serve warm.

ITALIAN SHRIMP SKEWERS

Simple and delicious mouthfuls from the Amalfi Coast.

2 pounds raw shrimp, peeled
¼ cup olive oil
3 tablespoons vegetable oil
1¼ cups very fine dry bread crumbs
1 garlic clove, crushed
1 tablespoon chopped fresh parsley
salt and ground black pepper
lemon wedges, to serve

SERVES 4

1 Slit the shrimp down their backs and remove the dark vein. Rinse in cold water and pat dry.

2 Put the olive oil and vegetable oil in a large bowl and add the shrimp, mixing them to coat evenly. Add the bread crumbs, garlic and parsley and season with salt and pepper. Toss the shrimp thoroughly to give them an even coating of bread crumbs. Cover and let marinate for at least 1 hour.

3 Thread the shrimp onto four metal or wooden skewers, curling them up as you do so, so that the tail is skewered in the middle.

4 Preheat the broiler. Place the skewers in the broiler pan and cook for about 2 minutes on each side, until the bread crumbs are golden. Serve with lemon wedges.

BLACK PASTA WITH SQUID SAUCE

Tagliatelle flavored with squid ink looks amazing and tastes deliciously of the sea. You'll find it at good Italian food stores.

7 tablespoons olive oil
2 shallots, chopped
3 garlic cloves, crushed
3 tablespoons chopped fresh parsley
1½ pounds cleaned squid, cut
into rings and rinsed
⅔ cup dry white wine
14-ounce can chopped tomatoes
½ teaspoon dried red pepper flakes
1 pound squid ink tagliatelle
salt and ground black pepper

SERVES 4

1 Heat the oil in a pan and add the shallots. Cook until pale golden, then add the garlic. When the garlic colors a little, add 2 tablespoons of the parsley, stir, then add the squid and stir again. Cook for 3–4 minutes, then add the wine.

2 Simmer for a few seconds, then add the tomatoes and red pepper flakes (*right*) and season with salt and pepper. Cover and simmer gently for about 1 hour, until the squid is tender. Add more water if necessary.

3 Cook the pasta in plenty of boiling salted water, according to the instructions on the package, or until al dente. Drain and return the tagliatelle to the pan. Add the squid sauce and mix well. Sprinkle each serving with the remaining chopped parsley and serve immediately.

SICILIAN SPAGHETTI WITH SARDINES

A traditional dish from Sicily, with ingredients that are common to many parts of the Mediterranean.

12 fresh sardines, cleaned and boned
1 cup olive oil
1 onion, chopped
¼ cup dill sprigs
½ cup pine nuts
2 tablespoons raisins, soaked in water
½ cup fresh bread crumbs
1 pound spaghetti
flour for dusting
salt

SERVES 4

 Wash the sardines and pat dry on paper towels. Open them out flat, then cut in half lengthwise.

2 Heat 2 tablespoons of the oil in a pan, add the onion and fry until golden. Add the dill and cook gently for a minute or two. Add the pine nuts and raisins and season with salt. Dry-fry the bread crumbs in a frying pan until golden. Set aside.

3 Cook the spaghetti in boiling salted water according to the instructions on the package until al dente. Heat the remaining oil in a pan. Dust the sardines with flour and fry in the hot oil for 2–3 minutes. Drain on paper towels.

4 Drain the spaghetti and return to the pan. Add the onion mixture and toss well. Transfer the spaghetti mixture to a serving platter and arrange the fried sardines on top. Sprinkle with the toasted bread crumbs and serve immediately.

GRILLED JUMBO SHRIMP WITH ROMESCO SAUCE

This sauce, from the Catalan region of Spain, is served with fish and shellfish. Its main ingredients are pimento, tomatoes, garlic and almonds.

24 raw jumbo shrimp
2–3 tablespoons olive oil
flat-leaf parsley, to garnish
lemon wedges, to serve

FOR THE SAUCE
2 ripe tomatoes
4 tablespoons olive oil
1 onion, chopped
4 garlic cloves, chopped
1 canned pimiento, chopped
½ teaspoon dried red pepper flakes
5 tablespoons fish stock
2 tablespoons white wine
10 blanched almonds
1 tablespoon red wine vinegar
salt

SERVES 4

1 To make the sauce, immerse the tomatoes in boiling water for about 30 seconds, then refresh them under cold water. Peel off the skins and coarsely chop the flesh.

2 Heat 2 tablespoons of the oil in a pan, add the onion and three-fourths of the chopped garlic and cook until soft. Add the pimiento, tomatoes, red pepper flakes, fish stock and wine, then cover and simmer for 30 minutes.

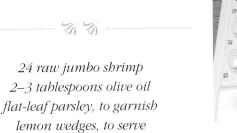

3 Toast the almonds under the broiler until golden. Transfer to a blender or food processor and grind coarsely. Add the remaining 2 tablespoons of oil, the vinegar and the remaining chopped garlic and process until evenly combined. Add the tomato and pimiento sauce and process until smooth. Season with salt.

4 Remove the heads from the shrimp, leaving them otherwise unshelled, and, with a sharp knife, slit each one down the back and remove the dark vein. Rinse and pat dry on paper towels. Preheat the broiler. Toss the shrimp in olive oil, then spread out in the broiler pan. Broil for 2–3 minutes on each side, until pink. Arrange on a serving platter with the lemon wedges, and place the sauce in a small bowl. Serve immediately, garnished with parsley.

GRILLED SEA BASS WITH FENNEL

This dish is served in almost every seafood restaurant on the French Mediterranean coast.
Traditionally, fennel twigs are used, but as they are hard to find, this recipe uses fennel seeds.

1 sea bass, weighing
4–4½ pounds, cleaned
4–6 tablespoons olive oil
2–3 teaspoons fennel seeds
2 large fennel bulbs, trimmed and
thinly sliced (reserve any fronds)
¼ cup Pernod
salt and ground black pepper

SERVES 6–8

1 With a sharp knife, make three or four deep cuts in both sides of the fish. Brush the fish with olive oil and season with salt and pepper. Sprinkle the fennel seeds in the stomach cavity and in the cuts. Set aside while you cook the fennel.

2 Preheat the broiler. Put the slices of fennel in an ovenproof dish or on the broiler rack and brush with oil. Broil for 4 minutes on each side, until tender. Transfer to a large platter.

3 Place the fish on the oiled broiler rack and position 4–5 inches away from the heat. Cook for 10–12 minutes on each side, brushing with oil occasionally.

4 Transfer the fish to the platter on top of the fennel. Garnish with fennel fronds. Heat the Pernod in a small pan, light it and pour it, flaming, over the fish. Serve immediately.

BRANDADE DE MORUE

Salt cod is popular in Spain and France, and it can be found cooked in a number of ways. This recipe is a purée flavored with garlic and olive oil that is made all over southern France.

1½ pounds salt cod
1¼ cups olive oil
1 cup milk
1 garlic clove, crushed
grated nutmeg
lemon juice, to taste
white pepper
parsley sprigs, to garnish

FOR THE CROUTONS
¼ cup olive oil
6 slices white bread, crusts removed
1 garlic clove, halved

SERVES 6

1. Soak the salt cod in cold water for at least 24 hours, changing the water several times. Drain.

2. To make the croutons, heat the oil in a frying pan. Cut the bread slices in half diagonally and fry in the hot oil until golden. Drain on paper towels, then rub both sides with garlic.

3. Put the cod in a large pan with enough cold water to cover. Cover and bring to a boil. Simmer gently for 8–10 minutes, until just tender. Drain and cool. Flake the fish and discard any skin and bones.

4. Heat the oil in a pan until very hot. In a separate pan, scald the milk. Transfer the fish to a blender or food processor and, with the motor running, slowly pour in the hot oil, followed by the milk, until the mixture is smooth and stiff. Transfer to a bowl and beat in the crushed garlic. Season with nutmeg, lemon juice and white pepper. Let the **brandade** cool and then chill until almost ready to serve.

5. Spoon the brandade into a shallow serving bowl and surround with the croutons. Garnish with parsley and serve cold.

MOUCLADE OF MUSSELS

This recipe is quite similar to Moules Marinière but has the additional flavoring of fennel and mild curry. Traditionally, the mussels are shelled and piled into scallop shells, but nothing beats a bowlful of steaming hot, garlicky mussels, served in their own glistening shells.

4½ pounds fresh mussels
1 cup dry white wine
good pinch of grated nutmeg
3 thyme sprigs
2 bay leaves
1 small onion, finely chopped
4 tablespoons butter
1 fennel bulb, thinly sliced
4 garlic cloves, crushed
½ teaspoon curry paste or powder
2 tablespoons all-purpose flour
⅔ cup heavy cream
ground black pepper
chopped fresh dill, to garnish

SERVES 6

1. Scrub the mussels, discarding any that are damaged or open ones that do not close when tapped with a knife.

2. Put the wine, nutmeg, thyme, bay leaves and onion in a large saucepan and bring just to a boil. Pour in the mussels and cover with a lid. Cook for 4–5 minutes, until the mussels have opened.

3. Drain the mussels, reserving all the juices. Discard any mussels that remain closed.

4. Melt the butter in a large clean pan and gently sauté the fennel slices and garlic for about 5 minutes, until softened.

5. Stir in the curry paste or powder and flour and cook for 1 minute. Remove from the heat and gradually blend in the cooking juices from the mussels. Return to the heat and cook, stirring, for 2 minutes.

6. Stir in the cream and a little pepper. Add the mussels to the pan and heat through for 2 minutes. Serve hot, garnished with dill.

VARIATION
Saffron is a popular addition to a mouclade. Soak ½ teaspoon saffron strands in a little boiling water and add to the sauce with the stock.

OCTOPUS AND RED WINE STEW

Unless you're happy to clean and prepare octopus for this Greek dish, buy one that's ready for cooking.

2 pounds prepared octopus
1 pound onions, sliced
2 bay leaves
1 pound ripe tomatoes
¼ cup olive oil
4 garlic cloves, crushed
1 teaspoon sugar
1 tablespoon chopped fresh oregano
or rosemary
2 tablespoons chopped fresh parsley
⅔ cup red wine
2 tablespoons red wine vinegar
chopped fresh herbs, to garnish
warm bread and pine nuts, to serve

SERVES 4

1 Put the octopus in a saucepan of gently simmering water with a quarter of the onions and the bay leaves. Cook gently for 1 hour.

2 While the octopus is cooking, plunge the tomatoes into boiling water for 30 seconds, then refresh in cold water. Peel off the skins and chop coarsely.

3 Drain the octopus and, using a sharp knife, cut it into bite-size pieces. Discard the head.

4 Heat the oil in a saucepan and sauté the octopus, the remaining onions and the garlic for 3 minutes. Add the tomatoes, sugar, oregano or rosemary, parsley, wine and vinegar and cook, stirring, for 5 minutes, until pulpy.

5 Cover the pan and cook over the lowest possible heat for about 1½ hours, until the sauce is thickened and the octopus is tender. Garnish with fresh herbs and serve with warm bread and pine nuts to sprinkle on top.

VARIATION
Use white wine instead of red and stir in ½ cup coarsely chopped black olives before serving.

FRESH TUNA AND TOMATO STEW

A deliciously simple dish that relies on good basic ingredients. For real Italian flavor, serve with polenta or pasta and an herb salad.

12 baby onions, peeled
2 pounds ripe tomatoes
1½ pounds fresh tuna
3 tablespoons olive oil
2 garlic cloves, crushed
3 tablespoons chopped fresh herbs
2 bay leaves
½ teaspoon sugar
2 tablespoons sun-dried tomato paste
⅔ cup dry white wine
salt and ground black pepper
baby zucchini and fresh herbs,
to garnish

SERVES 4

VARIATION

Two large mackerel make a nice alternative to the tuna. Fillet them and cut them into chunks or simply lay the whole fish on the sauce and cook, covered with a lid, until the mackerel is cooked through.

Sage, rosemary or oregano all go extremely well with this dish. Choose whichever you prefer, or use a mixture of one or two.

1 | Leave the onions whole and cook in a pan of boiling water for 4–5 minutes, until softened. Drain.

2 | Plunge the tomatoes into boiling water for 30 seconds, then refresh in cold water. Peel off the skins and chop coarsely.

3 | Cut the tuna into 1-inch chunks. Heat the oil in a large frying or sauté pan and quickly sauté the tuna until browned. Drain.

4 | Add the onions, garlic, tomatoes, chopped herbs, bay leaves, sugar, tomato paste and wine and bring to a boil, breaking up the tomatoes with a wooden spoon.

5 | Reduce the heat and simmer gently for 5 minutes. Return the fish to the pan and cook for another 5 minutes. Season and serve hot, garnished with baby zucchini and fresh herbs.

BRODETTO

The different regions of Italy have their own variations of this dish, but all require a good fish stock. Make sure you buy some of the fish whole so you can simply simmer them, remove the cooked flesh and strain the deliciously flavored juices to make the stock.

2 pounds mixed fish fillets or steaks,
such as monkfish, cod, haddock,
halibut or hake
2 pounds mixed conger eel, red or
gray mullet, snapper or small
white fish
1 onion, halved
1 celery stalk, coarsely chopped
½ pound squid
½ pound fresh mussels
1½ pounds ripe tomatoes
¼ cup olive oil
1 large onion, thinly sliced
3 garlic cloves, crushed
1 teaspoon saffron strands
⅔ cup dry white wine
6 tablespoons chopped fresh parsley
salt and ground black pepper
croutons, to serve

SERVES 4–5

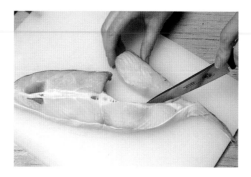

1 Remove any skin and bones from the fish fillets or steaks, cut the fish into large pieces and reserve. Place the bones in a pan with all the remaining fish.

2 Add the halved onion and the celery and just cover with water. Bring almost to a boil, then reduce the heat and simmer gently for about 30 minutes. Lift out the fish and remove the flesh from the bones. Reserve the stock.

3 To prepare the squid, twist the head and tentacles away from the body. Cut the head from the tentacles. Discard the body contents and peel off the mottled skin. Wash the tentacles and bodies and dry on paper towels.

COOK'S TIP
To make the croutons, cut thin slices from a long thin stick of bread and shallow-fry in a little butter until golden.

4 Scrub the mussels, discarding any that are damaged or open ones that do not close when tapped.

5 Plunge the tomatoes into boiling water for 30 seconds, then refresh in cold water. Peel off the skins and chop coarsely.

6 Heat the oil in a large saucepan or sauté pan. Add the sliced onion and the garlic and sauté gently for 3 minutes. Add the squid and the uncooked fish that you reserved earlier and sauté quickly on all sides. Drain.

7 Add 2 cups strained reserved fish stock, the saffron and tomatoes to the pan. Pour in the wine. Bring to a boil, then reduce the heat and simmer for about 5 minutes. Add the mussels, cover, and cook for 3–4 minutes, until the mussels have opened. Discard any that remain closed.

8 Season the sauce with salt and pepper and put all the fish in the pan. Cook gently for 5 minutes. Sprinkle on the parsley and serve with the croutons.

SARDINE GRATIN

In Sicily and other regions of the western Mediterranean, sardines are filled with a robust stuffing, flavorful enough to compete with the rich oiliness of the fish.

1 tablespoon light olive oil
½ small onion, finely chopped
2 garlic cloves, crushed
6 tablespoons blanched
    almonds, chopped
2 tablespoons golden raisins,
    coarsely chopped
10 pitted black olives
2 tablespoons capers, coarsely
    chopped
2 tablespoons coarsely chopped
    fresh parsley
1 cup bread crumbs
16 large sardines, scaled and gutted
⅓ cup grated Parmesan cheese
salt and ground black pepper
flat-leaf parsley, to garnish

SERVES 4

ABOVE: *Brodetto (top) and Sardine Gratin (bottom)*

 Preheat the oven to 400°F. Lightly oil a large, shallow ovenproof dish.

2 Heat the oil in a frying pan and sauté the onion and garlic gently for 3 minutes. Stir in the almonds, raisins, olives, capers, parsley and ¼ cup of the bread crumbs. Season lightly with salt and pepper.

3 Make 2–3 diagonal cuts on each side of the sardines. Pack the stuffing into the cavities and lay the sardines in the prepared dish.

4 Mix the remaining bread crumbs with the cheese and sprinkle on the fish. Bake for about 20 minutes, until the fish is cooked through. Test by piercing one sardine through the thickest part with a knife. Garnish with parsley and serve immediately, with a leafy salad.

ZARZUELA

Zarzuela means "light opera" or "musical comedy" in Spanish, and the classic fish stew of the same name should be as lively and colorful as the zarzuela itself. This feast of fish includes lobster and other shellfish, but you can modify the ingredients to suit the occasion and availability.

1 cooked lobster
24 fresh mussels or clams
1 large monkfish tail
8 ounces squid rings
1 tablespoon all-purpose flour
6 tablespoons olive oil
12 large raw shrimp
1 pound ripe tomatoes
2 large mild onions, chopped
4 garlic cloves, crushed
2 tablespoons brandy
2 bay leaves
1 teaspoon paprika
1 fresh red chile, seeded and chopped
1¼ cups fish stock
2 tablespoons ground almonds
2 tablespoons chopped fresh parsley
salt and ground black pepper

SERVES 6

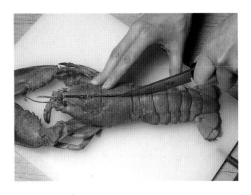

1   Using a large knife, cut the lobster in half lengthwise. Remove the dark intestine that runs down the length of the tail. Crack the claws using a hammer.

2   Scrub the mussels, discarding any that are damaged or open ones that do not close when tapped with a knife. Cut the monkfish fillets away from the central cartilage and cut each fillet into three pieces.

3   Toss the monkfish and squid in seasoned flour. Heat the oil in a large frying pan. Add the monkfish and squid and sauté quickly; remove from the pan. Sauté the shrimp on both sides, then remove from the pan.

4   Plunge the tomatoes into boiling water for 30 seconds, then refresh in cold water. Peel away the skins and chop coarsely.

5   Add the onions and two-thirds of the garlic to the frying pan and, stirring thoroughly, sauté for about 3 minutes. Add the brandy and ignite. When the flames die down, add the tomatoes, bay leaves, paprika, chile and stock.

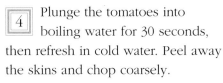

6   Bring to a boil, reduce the heat and simmer gently for 5 minutes. Add the mussels or clams, cover and cook for 3–4 minutes, until the shells have opened.

7   Remove the mussels or clams from the sauce and discard any that remain closed.

8   Arrange all the fish, including the lobster, in a large flameproof serving dish. Blend the ground almonds to a paste with the remaining garlic and parsley and stir into the sauce. Season with salt and pepper.

9   Pour the sauce over the fish and lobster and cook gently for about 5 minutes, until hot. Serve immediately with a green salad and plenty of warm bread.

BAKED FISH WITH TAHINI SAUCE

This North African recipe evokes all the color and rich flavors of Mediterranean cuisine. Choose any whole white fish, such as sea bass, hake, bream or snapper.

1 whole fish, about 2½ pounds, scaled
and cleaned
2 teaspoons coriander seeds
4 garlic cloves, sliced
2 teaspoons harissa
6 tablespoons olive oil
6 plum tomatoes, sliced
1 mild onion, sliced
3 preserved lemons or 1 fresh lemon
plenty of fresh herbs, such as bay
leaves, thyme and rosemary
salt and ground black pepper

FOR THE SAUCE
⅓ cup light tahini
juice of 1 lemon
1 garlic clove, crushed
3 tablespoons finely chopped fresh
parsley or cilantro
extra herbs, to garnish

SERVES 4

1 Preheat the oven to 400°F. Grease the bottom and sides of a large, shallow ovenproof dish or roasting pan.

2 Slash the fish diagonally on both sides with a sharp knife. Finely crush the coriander seeds and garlic with a mortar and pestle. Mix with the harissa and about 4 tablespoons of the olive oil.

3 Spread a little of the harissa, coriander and garlic paste inside the cavity of the fish. Spread the remainder over each side of the fish and set aside.

4 Scatter the tomatoes, onion and preserved or fresh lemon into the dish. (Thinly slice the lemon if using fresh.) Sprinkle with the remaining oil and season with salt and pepper. Lay the fish on top and tuck plenty of herbs around it.

5 Bake, uncovered, for about 25 minutes or until the fish has turned opaque—test by piercing the thickest part with a knife.

6 Meanwhile, make the sauce. Put the tahini, lemon juice, garlic and parsley or cilantro in a small saucepan with ½ cup water and add a little salt and pepper. Cook gently until smooth and heated through. Serve in a separate dish.

COOK'S TIP
If you can't get a suitable large fish, use small whole fish such as red snapper or even cod or haddock steaks. Remember to reduce the cooking time slightly.

STUFFED SQUID

This Greek delicacy is best made with large squid, because they are less awkward to stuff. If you have to make do with small squid, buy about 1 pound.

FOR THE STUFFING
2 tablespoons olive oil
1 large onion, finely chopped
2 garlic cloves, crushed
1 cup fresh bread crumbs
4 tablespoons chopped fresh parsley
4 ounces halloumi cheese, grated
salt and ground black pepper

TO FINISH
4 drained squid, each about
7 inches long
2 pounds ripe tomatoes
3 tablespoons olive oil
1 large onion, chopped
1 teaspoon sugar
½ cup dry white wine
several rosemary sprigs
toasted pine nuts and flat-leaf parsley,
to garnish

SERVES 4

1 To make the stuffing, heat the oil in a frying pan and sauté the onion for 3 minutes. Remove the pan from the heat and add the garlic, bread crumbs, parsley, cheese and a little salt and pepper. Stir until thoroughly blended.

2 Dry the squid on paper towels and fill with the prepared stuffing using a teaspoon. Secure the ends of the squid with wooden toothpicks.

VARIATION

If you would prefer a less rich filling, halve the quantity of cheese and bread crumbs in the stuffing and add 8 ounces cooked spinach.

3 Plunge the tomatoes into boiling water for 30 seconds, then refresh in cold water. Peel off the skins and chop coarsely.

4 Heat the oil in a frying pan or sauté pan. Add the squid and sauté on all sides. Remove from the pan.

5 Add the onion to the pan and sauté gently for 3 minutes. Stir in the tomatoes, sugar and wine and cook rapidly until the mixture becomes thick and pulpy.

6 Return the squid to the pan with the rosemary. Cover and cook gently for 30 minutes. Slice the squid and serve on individual plates with the sauce. Sprinkle the pine nuts on top and garnish with parsley.

HAKE AND CLAMS WITH SALSA VERDE

Hake (an Atlantic fish) is one of the most popular fish in Spain; here, it is cooked in a sauce flavored with parsley, lemon juice and garlic.

4 hake steaks, about ¾ inch thick
½ cup flour for dusting, plus
2 tablespoons
4 tablespoons olive oil
1 tablespoon lemon juice
1 small onion, finely chopped
4 garlic cloves, crushed
⅔ cup fish stock
⅔ cup white wine
6 tablespoons chopped fresh parsley
3 ounces frozen tiny peas
16 fresh clams
salt and ground black pepper

SERVES 4

1 Preheat the oven to 350°F. Season the fish with salt and pepper, then dust both sides with flour. Heat 2 tablespoons of the oil in a large sauté pan, add the fish and sauté for about 1 minute on each side. Transfer to an ovenproof dish and sprinkle with lemon juice.

2 Clean the pan, then heat the remaining oil. Add the onion and garlic and cook until soft. Stir in 2 tablespoons flour and cook for about 1 minute. Gradually add the stock and wine, stirring until thickened and smooth. Add 5 tablespoons of the parsley and the peas and season with salt and pepper.

3 Pour the sauce over the fish and bake for 15–20 minutes, adding the clams to the dish 3–4 minutes before the end of the cooking time. Discard any clams that do not open, then sprinkle with the remaining parsley before serving.

COD PLAKI

This is a traditional Greek preparation for fish, using onions, tomatoes, parsley and olive oil. Although cod is an Atlantic fish, it works very well in this recipe.

1¼ cups olive oil
2 onions, thinly sliced
3 large ripe tomatoes, coarsely chopped
3 garlic cloves, thinly sliced
1 teaspoon sugar
1 teaspoon chopped fresh dill
1 teaspoon chopped fresh mint
1 teaspoon chopped fresh celery leaves
1 tablespoon chopped fresh parsley
6 cod steaks
juice of 1 lemon
salt and ground black pepper
extra dill, mint or parsley, to garnish

SERVES 6

1   Heat the oil in a large sauté pan or flameproof dish. Add the onions and cook until pale golden. Add the tomatoes, garlic, sugar, dill, mint, celery leaves and parsley with 1¼ cups water. Season with salt and pepper, then simmer, uncovered, for 25 minutes, until the liquid has reduced by one-third.

2   Add the fish steaks and cook gently for 10–12 minutes, until the fish is just cooked. Remove from the heat and add the lemon juice (*left*). Cover and let stand for about 20 minutes before serving. Arrange the cod in a dish and spoon the sauce over. Garnish with herbs and serve warm or cold.

MEAT

*The Mediterranean style of cooking makes the
most of young lamb and pork, while tougher cuts
are slow-cooked in superb sauces.*

Unlike the vegetable and fish recipes from the Mediterranean, meat recipes do not readily spring to mind. The countryside around the Mediterranean can be quite harsh—no lush, green fields for animals to graze. Beasts are often slaughtered young, and baby lamb and goat are favorite meats. Traditionally, these animals were usually roasted whole on a spit, flavored with wild herbs, and eaten on feast days. The meat of the young kid is particularly popular in certain parts of the Mediterranean, such as Corsica, parts of Greece and the Middle East. Cattle are a rare sight and, in times past, beef was considered a luxury. Many rural families kept a pig, which was slaughtered and the meat preserved, to feed them through the chilly winter months. This, in turn, inspired the many wonderful dry sausages, like salami, and the cured hams, which are still popular today, and appreciated all over the world. Both Jews and Muslims were forbidden by their religion to eat pork, so there are no traditional pork recipes from their countries and regions.

ABOVE: Sunlight dapples the walls of this farmhouse overlooking Lake Trasimeno, in Umbria.

In the Middle East, only lamb and mutton were eaten, although nowadays beef and veal are becoming more popular. The Roman Catholic and Greek Orthodox Churches used to have strict rules concerning "lean" days, when meat could not be consumed, and therefore many special feast dishes using meat were created to celebrate the ends of these regular fasts.

Meat was often of poor quality if the beast had not been properly fed, resulting in tough and stringy cuts. This was remedied by marinating the meat in wine or yogurt and cooking it slowly at a low temperature, to tenderize it and improve the flavor. These methods resulted in some of the most delicious recipes for casseroles and stews. Many are still cooked today, despite the fact that the meat is probably of better quality. Daubes from France, tagines from Morocco, estofados

RIGHT: This French shepherd has a magnificent view of the Provençal countryside.

BELOW: Sacks of spices and grains invite inspection at a Tunisian market.

from Spain—every country has its own version, recipes having been handed down through the generations. As meat was a luxury, beans, rice and potatoes were often added to the pot to make the meal go further.

Another popular method of cooking meat is broiling. Quite often the meat is threaded onto skewers, or sometimes a branch of rosemary or bay, with chunks of onion and other vegetables. This is a basic form of cooking, originating from cooking over the hot embers of an open fire, and it results in succulent, smoky-flavored meat. Greece and the Middle East have mastered this technique, and the smell of meat cooking on a wood fire is one associated with these countries. Using ground meat, in

the form of patties, meatballs, sausages, sauces for pasta and fillings for savory pastries, is popular throughout the Mediterranean. This was another way of padding out meat with other ingredients to make a more economical dish. Bread crumbs, rice, bulgur and potatoes are all used to add more bulk, particularly when making meatballs and patties. Onion and tomatoes give flavor and volume to sauces. In the Middle East, spices, nuts and dried fruits are often mixed with ground meat, to make delicious fillings for little parcels of phyllo. Elsewhere, in Italy, garlic, wine, and herbs are added to slow-cooked meat sauces, to eat with pasta. In Greece, ground lamb is layered with eggplant, tomato sauce and béchamel sauce to create Moussaka, and in Turkey, ground lamb is used to stuff halved eggplant, the vegetable flesh being mixed with the ground meat. These versatile dishes are good for feeding a large crowd, often making a little go a long way.

Although there are no recipes for goat in this chapter (as it is not readily available), the selection varies from Sicilian Pork with Marsala to Turkish Lamb Pilaf and Greek Lamb Sausages with Tomato Sauce. As with most recipes in this book, all that is needed to accompany any of them, once cooked and ready to eat, is a glass of wine (in this case red) and some good bread!

TURKISH LAMB PILAF

Here we have a delicious combination of rice, lamb, spices, nuts and fruit—a typical Middle Eastern dish.

3 tablespoons butter
1 large onion, finely chopped
1 pound lamb fillet, cut into
small cubes
½ teaspoon ground cinnamon
2 tablespoons tomato paste
3 tablespoons chopped fresh parsley
½ cup dried apricots, halved
¾ cup pistachios
1 pound long-grain rice, rinsed
salt and ground black pepper
flat-leaf parsley, to garnish

SERVES 4

1 | Heat the butter in a large, heavy pan. Add the onion and cook until soft and golden. Add the cubed lamb and brown on all sides. Add the cinnamon and season with salt and pepper. Cover and cook gently for 10 minutes.

2 | Add the tomato paste and enough water to cover the meat. Stir in the parsley, bring to a boil, cover and simmer very gently for 1½ hours, until the meat is tender. Chop the pistachios.

3 | Add enough water to the pan to measure about 2½ cups liquid. Add the apricots, pistachios and rice, bring to a boil, cover tightly and simmer for about 20 minutes, until the rice is cooked. (You may need to add a little more water.) Transfer to a warmed serving dish and garnish with parsley before serving.

GREEK LAMB SAUSAGES WITH TOMATO SAUCE

The Greek name for these sausages is "soudzoukakia." They are more like elongated meatballs than the sausage shapes we are accustomed to. Passata is strained tomato pulp, which can be bought in cartons or jars.

1 cup fresh bread crumbs

⅔ cup milk

1½ pounds ground lamb

2 tablespoons grated onion

3 garlic cloves, crushed

2 teaspoons ground cumin

2 tablespoons chopped fresh parsley

flour for dusting

olive oil for frying

2½ cups passata

1 teaspoon sugar

2 bay leaves

1 small onion, peeled

salt and ground black pepper

flat-leaf parsley, to garnish

SERVES 4

1 Combine the bread crumbs and milk. Add the lamb, onion, garlic, cumin and parsley and season with salt and pepper.

2 Shape the mixture with your hands into little fat sausages, about 2 inches long, and roll them in flour. Heat about ¼ cup olive oil in a frying pan.

3 Fry the sausages for about 8 minutes, turning them until evenly browned. Remove and place on paper towels to drain.

4 Put the passata, sugar, bay leaves and whole onion in a pan and simmer for 20 minutes. Add the sausages and cook for 10 more minutes. Serve garnished with parsley.

MEAT

ROAST LOIN OF PORK STUFFED WITH FIGS, OLIVES AND ALMONDS

Pork is a popular meat in Spain, and this recipe using fruit and nuts in the stuffing is inspired by Catalan cooking, where the combination of meat and fruit is quite common.

4 tablespoons olive oil
1 onion, finely chopped
2 garlic cloves, chopped
1½ cups fresh bread crumbs
4 dried figs, chopped
8 pitted green olives, chopped
¼ cup sliced almonds
1 tablespoon lemon juice
1 tablespoon chopped fresh parsley
1 egg yolk
2 pounds boned loin of pork
salt and ground black pepper

SERVES 4

1 Preheat the oven to 400°F. Heat 3 tablespoons of the oil in a pan, add the onion and garlic, and cook gently until softened. Remove the pan from the heat and stir in the bread crumbs, figs, olives, almonds, lemon juice, parsley and egg yolk. Season to taste.

COOK'S TIP
Keep a container of bread crumbs in the freezer. They can be used frozen.

2 Remove any string from the pork and unroll the belly flap, cutting away any excess fat or meat to enable you to do so. Spread half the stuffing on the flat piece and roll up, starting from the thick side. Tie at intervals with string.

3 Pour the remaining oil into a small roasting pan and put in the pork. Roast for 1 hour and 15 minutes. Form the remaining stuffing mixture into balls and add to the roasting pan around the meat 15–20 minutes before the end of cooking time.

4 Remove the pork from the oven and let it rest for 10 minutes. Carve into thick slices and serve with the stuffing balls and any juices from the pan. This is also good served cold.

LAMB WITH RED PEPPERS AND RIOJA

Plenty of garlic, bell peppers, herbs and red wine give this lamb stew a lovely, rich flavor. Slice through the pepper stems, rather than removing them, as this makes it look extra special.

2 pounds lean lamb fillet
1 tablespoon all-purpose flour
¼ cup olive oil
2 red onions, sliced
4 garlic cloves, sliced
2 teaspoons paprika
¼ teaspoon ground cloves
1⅔ cups red Rioja wine
⅔ cup lamb stock
2 bay leaves
2 thyme sprigs
3 red bell peppers, halved and seeded
salt and ground black pepper
bay leaves and thyme sprigs,
to garnish
green beans and saffron rice or boiled
potatoes, to serve

SERVES 4

1 Preheat the oven to 325°F. Cut the lamb into chunks. Season the flour, add the lamb and toss lightly to coat.

2 Heat the oil in a frying pan and sauté the lamb, stirring, until browned. Transfer to an ovenproof dish. Lightly sauté the onions in the pan with the garlic, paprika and cloves.

VARIATION
Use lean cubed pork instead of the lamb and a white Rioja wine instead of the red. A mixture of red, yellow and orange bell peppers looks very effective.

3 Add the Rioja, stock, bay leaves and thyme and bring to a boil, stirring. Pour the contents of the pan onto the meat. Cover with a lid and bake for 30 minutes.

4 Remove the dish from the oven. Stir the red peppers into the stew and season lightly with salt and pepper. Bake for another 30 minutes, until the meat is tender. Garnish the stew with bay leaves and sprigs of thyme and serve with green beans and saffron rice or boiled potatoes.

CORSICAN BEEF STEW WITH MACARONI

Pasta is eaten in many parts of the Mediterranean. In Corsica, it's often served with gravy as a sauce and, in this case, in a rich beef stew.

1 ounce dried mushrooms
(cèpes or porcini)
6 garlic cloves
2 pounds stewing beef, cut into
2-inch cubes
4 ounces lardons, or thick bacon
cut into strips
3 tablespoons olive oil
2 onions, sliced
1¼ cups dry white wine
2 tablespoons passata
(or tomato sauce)
pinch of ground cinnamon
sprig of rosemary
1 bay leaf
2 cups large macaroni
⅔ cup freshly grated
Parmesan cheese
salt and ground black pepper

SERVES 4

1 Soak the dried mushrooms in warm water for 30 minutes. Drain, set the mushrooms aside and reserve the liquid. Cut three of the garlic cloves into thin strips and insert into the pieces of beef by making little slits with a sharp knife. Push the lardons or pieces of bacon into the beef with the garlic. Season the meat with salt and pepper.

3 Stir in the white wine, passata, mushrooms, cinnamon, rosemary and bay leaf and season with salt and pepper. Cook gently for about 30 minutes, stirring often. Strain the mushroom liquid and add to the stew with enough water to cover. Bring to a boil, cover and simmer very gently for 3 hours, until the meat is very tender.

2 Heat the oil in a heavy pan, add half the beef and brown well on all sides. Repeat with the remaining beef. Transfer to a plate. Add the sliced onions to the pan and cook until lightly browned. Crush the remaining garlic and add to the onions with the meat.

4 Cook the macaroni in a large pan of boiling salted water for 10 minutes or until al dente Lift the pieces of meat out of the gravy and transfer to a warmed serving platter. Drain the pasta and layer in a serving bowl with the gravy and cheese. Serve with the meat.

AFELIA

This lightly spiced pork stew makes a delicious supper dish served simply, as it would be in Cyprus, with warm bread, a leafy salad and a few olives.

3 Preheat the oven to 325°F. Heat 2 tablespoons of the oil in a frying pan over high heat. Brown the meat quickly, then transfer to an ovenproof dish.

1½ pounds pork fillet, boneless leg or loin chops
4 teaspoons coriander seeds
½ teaspoon sugar
3 tablespoons olive oil
2 large onions, sliced
1¼ cups red wine
salt and ground black pepper
cilantro, to garnish

SERVES 4

COOK'S TIP
A clean coffee grinder can also be used to grind the coriander seeds. Alternatively, use 1 tablespoon ground coriander.

1 Cut the pork into small chunks, discarding any excess fat. Crush the coriander seeds with a mortar and pestle until fairly finely ground.

2 Mix the coriander seeds with the sugar and salt and pepper and rub all over the meat. Let marinate for up to 4 hours.

4 Add the remaining oil to the pan and sauté the onions until beginning to color. Stir in the wine and a little salt and pepper and bring just to a boil.

5 Pour the onion and wine mixture over the meat and cover with a lid. Bake for 1 hour or until the meat is very tender. Serve sprinkled with cilantro.

MOUSSAKA

Like many popular classics, a real moussaka bears little resemblance to the imitations experienced in many Greek tourist resorts. This one is mildly spiced, moist but not dripping in grease, and encased in a golden baked crust.

2 pounds eggplant
½ cup olive oil
2 large tomatoes
2 large onions, sliced
1 pound ground lamb
¼ teaspoon ground cinnamon
¼ teaspoon ground allspice
2 tablespoons tomato paste
3 tablespoons chopped fresh parsley
½ cup dry white wine
salt and ground black pepper

FOR THE SAUCE
4 tablespoons butter
½ cup all-purpose flour
2½ cups milk
¼ teaspoon grated nutmeg
⅓ cup grated Parmesan cheese
3 tablespoons toasted bread crumbs

SERVES 6

1   Cut the eggplant into ¼-inch thick slices. Layer the slices in a colander, sprinkling each layer with plenty of salt. Let stand for 30 minutes.

2   Rinse the eggplant in several changes of cold water. Squeeze gently with your fingers to remove the excess water, then pat them dry on paper towels.

3   Heat some of the oil in a large frying pan. Sauté the eggplant slices in batches until golden on both sides, adding more oil when necessary. Let the eggplant slices drain on paper towels.

4   Plunge the tomatoes into boiling water for 30 seconds, then refresh in cold water. Peel away the skins and chop coarsely.

5   Preheat the oven to 350°F. Heat 2 tablespoons oil in a saucepan. Add the onions and lamb and sauté gently for 5 minutes, stirring and breaking up the lamb with a wooden spoon.

VARIATION
Sliced and sautéed zucchini or potatoes can be used instead of the eggplant in this dish.

6   Add the tomatoes, cinnamon, allspice, tomato paste, parsley, wine and pepper and bring to a boil. Reduce the heat, cover with a lid and simmer gently for 15 minutes.

7   Spoon alternate layers of the eggplant and meat mixture into a shallow ovenproof dish, finishing with a layer of eggplant.

8   To make the sauce, melt the butter in a small pan and stir in the flour. Cook, stirring, for 1 minute. Remove from the heat and gradually blend in the milk. Return to the heat and cook, stirring, for 2 minutes, until thickened. Add the nutmeg, cheese and salt and pepper. Pour the sauce on the eggplant and sprinkle with the bread crumbs. Bake for 45 minutes, until golden. Serve hot, sprinkled with extra black pepper, if desired.

BEEF ROLLS WITH GARLIC AND TOMATO SAUCE

*Italy has many regional variations on the technique of wrapping thin slices of beef around a richly
flavored stuffing. This recipe incorporates some classic ingredients. Serve with polenta, if desired.*

4 thin slices of sirloin steak (about
4 ounces each)
4 slices smoked ham
5 ounces Pecorino cheese, grated
2 garlic cloves, crushed
5 tablespoons chopped fresh parsley
2 eggs, soft-boiled and peeled
3 tablespoons olive oil
1 large onion, finely chopped
⅔ cup passata or tomato sauce
⅓ cup red wine
2 bay leaves
⅔ cup beef stock
salt and ground black pepper
flat-leaf parsley, to garnish

SERVES 4

1. Preheat the oven to 325°F. Lay the steak slices on a sheet of waxed paper. Cover the steak with another sheet of waxed paper or plastic wrap and beat with a mallet or rolling pin until the slices are very thin.

2. Lay a ham slice over each. Mix the cheese in a bowl with the garlic, parsley, eggs and a little salt and pepper. Stir well until all the ingredients are evenly mixed.

3. Spoon the stuffing onto the ham and steak slices. Fold two opposite sides of the meat over the stuffing, then roll up the meat to form neat parcels. Secure with string.

4. Heat the oil in a frying pan. Add the parcels and sauté quickly on all sides to brown. Transfer to an ovenproof dish.

5. Add the onion to the frying pan and sauté for 3 minutes. Stir in the passata, wine, bay leaves and stock and season with salt and pepper. Bring to a boil, then pour the sauce over the meat in the dish.

6. Cover the dish and bake for 1 hour. Drain the meat and remove the string. Spoon onto warmed serving plates. Taste the sauce, adding extra salt and pepper if necessary, and spoon it over the meat. Serve garnished with flat-leaf parsley.

PORK WITH MARSALA WINE AND JUNIPER

Although most frequently used in desserts, Sicilian marsala gives savory dishes a rich, fruity tang.
Use good quality butcher's pork that won't be drowned out by the flavor of the sauce.

1 ounce dried cèpes or porcini
mushrooms
4 pork cutlets
2 teaspoons balsamic vinegar
8 garlic cloves
1 tablespoon butter
3 tablespoons marsala wine
several rosemary sprigs
10 juniper berries, crushed
salt and ground black pepper
noodles and green vegetables,
to serve

SERVES 4

1 Put the dried mushrooms in a bowl and just cover with hot water. Let stand.

2 Brush the pork with 1 teaspoon of the vinegar and season with salt and pepper. Put the garlic cloves in a small pan of boiling water and cook for 10 minutes, until soft. Drain and set aside.

3 Melt the butter in a large frying pan. Add the pork and cook quickly until browned on the underside. Turn the meat over and cook for another minute.

4 Add the marsala, rosemary, mushrooms, 4 tablespoons of the mushroom juices, the garlic cloves, juniper and remaining vinegar.

5 Simmer gently for about 3 minutes, until the pork is cooked through. Season lightly and serve hot with noodles and green vegetables.

SKEWERED LAMB WITH CILANTRO YOGURT

Although lamb is the most commonly used meat for Turkish kebabs, lean beef or pork work equally well.
For color you can alternate pieces of bell pepper, lemon or onions, although this is not traditional.

2 pounds lean boneless lamb
1 large onion, grated
3 bay leaves
5 thyme or rosemary sprigs
grated zest and juice of
1 lemon
½ teaspoon sugar
⅓ cup olive oil
salt and ground black pepper
sprigs of rosemary, to garnish
broiled lemon wedges, to serve

FOR THE CORIANDER YOGURT
⅔ cup thick plain yogurt
1 tablespoon chopped fresh mint
1 tablespoon chopped cilantro
2 teaspoons grated onion

SERVES 4

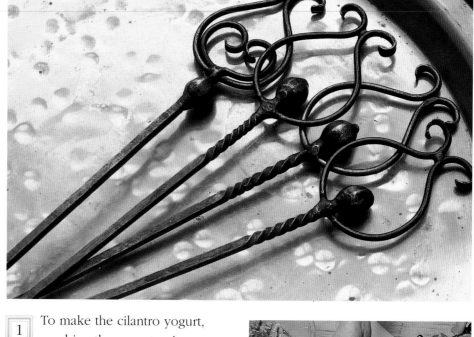

1 To make the cilantro yogurt, combine the yogurt, mint, cilantro and grated onion and transfer to a small serving dish.

2 To make the kebabs, cut the lamb into small chunks and put in a bowl. Combine the grated onion, herbs, lemon zest and juice, sugar and oil, then add salt and pepper and pour over the lamb.

3 Combine the ingredients and let marinate in the refrigerator for several hours or overnight.

4 Drain the meat and thread onto skewers. Arrange on a broiler rack and cook under a preheated broiler for about 10 minutes, until browned, turning occasionally. Transfer to a plate and garnish with rosemary. Serve with the broiled lemon wedges and the cilantro yogurt.

COOK'S TIP
Cover the tips of wooden skewers with foil so they don't char.

BLACK BEAN STEW

This simple Spanish stew uses a few robust ingredients to create a deliciously intense flavor, something like a French cassoulet.

1⅓ cups black beans
1½ pounds bacon
¼ cup olive oil
12 ounces baby onions
2 celery stalks, thickly sliced
2 teaspoons paprika
5 ounces chorizo sausage, cut into chunks
2½ cups light chicken or vegetable stock
2 green bell peppers, seeded and cut into large pieces
salt and ground black pepper

SERVES 5–6

1 Put the beans in a bowl and cover with plenty of cold water. Let soak overnight. Drain the beans in a saucepan and cover with fresh water. Bring to a boil and boil rapidly for 10 minutes. Drain.

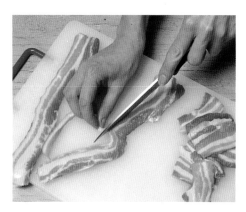

2 Preheat the oven to 325°F. Cut the bacon into chunks.

3 Heat the oil in a large frying pan and sauté the onions and celery for 3 minutes. Add the bacon and sauté for 5–10 minutes, until the bacon is browned.

4 Add the paprika and chorizo and cook for another 2 minutes. Transfer to an ovenproof dish with the beans and combine.

5 Add the stock to the pan and bring to a boil. Season lightly, then pour over the meat and beans. Cover and bake for 1 hour.

6 Stir the green peppers into the stew and return to the oven for 15 minutes more. Serve hot.

COOK'S TIP
This is the sort of stew to which you can add a variety of winter vegetables, such as chunks of leek, turnip, celery root and even little potatoes.

PROVENÇAL BEEF AND OLIVE DAUBE

A daube is a French method of braising meat with wine and herbs. This version from the Nice area in the south of France also includes black olives and tomatoes.

3–3½ pounds top round roast
½ pound lardons, or thick bacon cut into strips
½ pound carrots, sliced
1 bay leaf
1 thyme sprig
2 parsley sprigs
3 garlic cloves
2 cups pitted black or green olives
14-ounce can chopped tomatoes
crusty bread, flageolet beans or pasta, to serve

FOR THE MARINADE
½ cup extra virgin olive oil
1 onion, sliced
4 shallots, sliced
1 celery stalk, sliced
1 carrot, sliced
⅔ cup red wine
6 peppercorns
2 garlic cloves, sliced
1 bay leaf
1 thyme sprig
2 parsley stalks
salt

SERVES 6

1 To make the marinade, heat the oil in a large shallow pan and add the onion, shallots, celery and carrot. Cook for 2 minutes, then lower the heat and add the red wine, pepper-corns, garlic, bay leaf, thyme and parsley. Season with salt, then cover and let simmer gently for 15–20 minutes. Set aside.

3 Preheat the oven to 325°F. Lift the meat out of the marinade and fit snugly into an ovenproof casserole. Add the lardons or bacon and carrots, along with the herbs and garlic. Strain in all the marinade. Cover the casserole with waxed paper, then the lid, and bake for 2½ hours.

2 Place the beef in a large glass or earthenware dish and pour the cooled marinade over. Cover the dish and let marinate in a cool place or in the refrigerator for 12 hours, turning the meat once or twice.

4 Remove the casserole from the oven and stir in the olives and tomatoes. Re-cover the casserole, return to the oven and cook for another 30 minutes. Serve the meat cut into thick slices, accompanied by crusty bread, beans or pasta.

LAMB CASSEROLE WITH GARLIC AND FAVA BEANS

This recipe has a Spanish influence and makes a substantial meal, served with potatoes. It's based on stewing lamb with a large amount of garlic and sherry—the addition of fava beans gives color.

2 Heat the remaining oil in the pan, add the onion and cook for about 5 minutes, until soft. Return the meat to the casserole.

3 Add the garlic cloves, bay leaf, paprika and sherry. Season with salt and pepper. Bring to a boil, then cover and simmer very gently for 1½–2 hours, until the meat is tender.

4 Add the fava beans about 10 minutes before the end of the cooking time. Stir in the parsley just before serving.

3 tablespoons olive oil
3–3½ pounds lamb fillet, cut into
2-inch cubes
1 large onion, chopped
6 large garlic cloves, unpeeled
1 bay leaf
1 teaspoon paprika
½ cup dry sherry
4 ounces shelled fresh or frozen
fava beans
2 tablespoons chopped fresh parsley
salt and ground black pepper

SERVES 6

1 Heat 2 tablespoons of the oil in a large flameproof casserole. Add half the meat and brown well on all sides. Transfer to a plate. Brown the rest of the meat in the same way and remove from the casserole.

SPANISH PORK AND SAUSAGE CASSEROLE

Another pork dish from the Catalan region of Spain, which uses the spicy butifarra sausage. You can find these sausages in some Spanish food stores but, if not, sweet Italian sausages will do.

2 tablespoons olive oil
4 boneless pork chops, about
1 pound
4 butifarra or sweet Italian sausages
1 onion, chopped
2 garlic cloves, chopped
½ cup dry white wine
4 plum tomatoes, chopped
1 bay leaf
2 tablespoons chopped fresh parsley
salt and ground black pepper
green salad and baked potatoes,
to serve

SERVES 4

1 Heat the oil in a large, deep frying pan. Cook the pork chops over high heat until browned on both sides, then transfer to a plate.

2 Add the sausages, onion and garlic to the pan and cook over medium heat until the sausages are browned and the onion softened, turning the sausages two or three times during cooking. Return the chops to the pan.

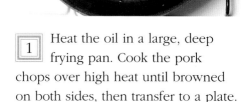

3 Stir in the wine, tomatoes and bay leaf, and season with salt and pepper. Add the parsley. Cover the pan and cook for 30 minutes.

4 Remove the sausages from the pan and cut them into thick slices. Return them to the pan and heat through. Serve hot, accompanied by a green salad and baked potatoes.

COOK'S TIP
Vine tomatoes, which are making a welcome appearance in supermarkets, can be used instead of plum tomatoes.

MEATBALLS WITH MOZZARELLA AND TOMATO

These Italian meatballs are made with beef and topped with mozzarella cheese and tomato.

½ *slice white bread, crusts removed*

3 tablespoons milk

1½ pounds ground beef

1 egg, beaten

⅔ *cup dry bread crumbs*

vegetable oil for frying

*2 beefsteak or other large
tomatoes, sliced*

1 tablespoon chopped fresh oregano

1 mozzarella cheese, cut into 6 slices

*6 drained canned anchovies, cut in
half lengthwise*

salt and ground black pepper

SERVES 6

1   Preheat the oven to 400°F. Put the bread and milk in a small saucepan and heat very gently over low heat until the bread absorbs all the milk. Mash it to a pulp and let cool.

2   Put the beef into a bowl with the bread mixture and the egg and season with salt and pepper. Mix well, then shape the mixture into six patties. Sprinkle the bread crumbs on a plate and dredge the patties, coating them thoroughly.

3   Heat about ¼ inch oil in a large frying pan. Add the patties and fry for 2 minutes on each side, until brown. Transfer to a greased ovenproof dish in a single layer.

4   Lay a slice of tomato on top of each patty, sprinkle with oregano and season with salt and pepper. Place the mozzarella slices on top. Arrange two strips of anchovy placed in a cross on top of each slice of mozzarella.

5   Bake for 10–15 minutes, until the mozzarella has melted. Serve hot, straight from the dish.

POULTRY
AND GAME

Poultry and game play key roles in the cuisines of all Mediterranean countries, and the addition of fruits creates sensational flavor combinations.

Poultry and game have always played an important role in Mediterranean cooking. This is largely due to the dry, rugged and, in some places, mountainous land that does not provide good pasture. Chickens and ducks are more accessible to the poorer people of the Mediterranean, who often raise them on their own land.

Chicken is without doubt the most popular type of poultry and is used creatively for Mediterranean dishes. Traditionally corn-fed, the poultry's flesh is rich in color and full of flavor, despite the fact that individual birds might look quite thin. The cooking methods are varied and interesting, but they have many similarities. In both the east and west Mediterranean cooks have acknowledged the fact that chicken is perfectly complemented by the tang of fresh, dried or preserved fruits, the rich earthiness of nuts and the lively warmth of spices.

In the Middle East, chickens were traditionally kept mainly for their eggs rather than meat, and generally only the older birds were cooked. This meant long, slow braising with highly flavored stuffings and sauces to add flavor. These recipes are now perfectly suited to improving the

BELOW: Verdant farmland rimmed by mountains in southern Spain.

RIGHT: Lord of all he surveys, this Greek cockerel patrols his perimeter wall.

BELOW: Lemons are a favorite flavoring for chicken dishes, notably in Chicken with Lemons and Olives.

mild taste of our mass-produced chickens. Preserved lemons tucked in or around a whole chicken impart a fresh, aromatic flavor that lacks the acidity of fresh lemons, although these can also be used successfully, adding a little sugar or honey for sweetness. Another popular flavoring for chicken is provided by glassy, jewellike segments of pomegranates, crushed and blended to a juice or made into a canned preserve, having been mixed with lemon, sugar and seasoning.

From the simplest roast, served with a raisin, pine nut and sherry sauce, to chorizo-flavored casseroles, Spain has numerous excellent chicken and rabbit recipes that are popular favorites throughout the country. Duck and goose feature prominently, cooked with pears, apples or figs to counteract the richness of the meat.

Small game birds are typically Mediterranean but are used more in winter, when the tourists have left. Squab and small game birds such as partridge and quail take their migratory route across the sea, and hunters from all quarters of the Mediterranean take full advantage of this. Italians are particularly fond of small game and prepare some delicious squab dishes, lightly cooked in rich sauces and accompanied by broiled or soft polenta.

CHICKEN THIGHS WITH LEMON AND GARLIC

This recipe uses classic flavorings for chicken. Versions of it can be found in Spain and Italy.
This particular recipe, however, is of French origin.

2½ cups chicken stock
20 large garlic cloves
2 tablespoons butter
1 tablespoon olive oil
8 chicken thighs
1 lemon, peeled, pith removed and
thinly sliced
2 tablespoons all-purpose flour
⅔ cup dry white wine
salt and ground black pepper
chopped fresh parsley or basil,
to garnish
new potatoes or rice, to serve

SERVES 4

1   Put the stock into a pan and bring to a boil. Add the garlic cloves, cover and simmer gently for 40 minutes. Heat the butter and oil in a sauté or frying pan, add the chicken thighs and cook gently on all sides until golden. Transfer them to an ovenproof dish. Preheat the oven to 375°F.

2   Strain the stock and reserve it. Distribute the garlic and lemon slices among the chicken pieces. Add the flour to the fat in the pan in which the chicken was browned and cook, stirring, for 1 minute. Add the wine, stirring constantly and scraping the bottom of the pan, then add the stock. Cook, stirring, until the sauce has thickened and is smooth. Season with salt and pepper.

3   Pour the sauce over the chicken, cover and bake for 40–45 minutes. If a thicker sauce is required, lift out the chicken pieces and reduce the sauce by boiling rapidly until it reaches the desired consistency. Sprinkle the chopped parsley or basil on top and serve with boiled new potatoes or rice.

OLIVE OIL-ROASTED CHICKEN WITH MEDITERRANEAN VEGETABLES

This is a delicious French alternative to a traditional roast chicken. Use a corn-fed or free-range bird, if available. This recipe also works well with guinea fowl.

4½-pound roasting chicken
⅔ cup extra virgin olive oil
½ lemon
few sprigs of fresh thyme
1 pound small new potatoes
1 eggplant, cut into 1-inch cubes
1 red bell pepper, seeded and
quartered
1 fennel bulb, trimmed and quartered
8 large garlic cloves, unpeeled
coarse salt and ground black pepper

SERVES 4

2 Remove the chicken from the oven and season with salt. Turn the chicken right side up and baste with the drippings from the pan. Surround the bird with the potatoes, roll them in the pan drippings and return the roasting pan to the oven to continue roasting.

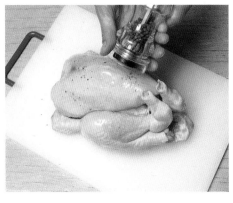

1 Preheat the oven to 400°F. Rub the chicken all over with olive oil and season with pepper. Place the lemon half inside the bird with a sprig or two of thyme. Put the chicken breast side down in a large roasting pan. Roast for about 30 minutes.

3 After 30 minutes, add the eggplant, red pepper, fennel and garlic cloves to the pan. Drizzle with the remaining oil and season with salt and pepper. Add any remaining thyme to the vegetables. Return to the oven and cook for 30–50 more minutes, basting and turning the vegetables occasionally.

4 To find out if the chicken is cooked, push the tip of a sharp knife between the thigh and breast. If the juices run clear, it is done. The vegetables should be tender and just beginning to brown. Serve the chicken and vegetables from the pan, or transfer the vegetables to a serving dish, cut up the chicken and place it on top. Serve the skimmed juices in a gravy boat.

CHICKEN WITH CHORIZO

The addition of chorizo sausage and sherry gives a warm, interesting flavor to this simple Spanish casserole. Serve with rice or boiled potatoes.

*1 medium chicken, cut up, or
4 chicken legs, halved
2 teaspoons ground paprika
4 tablespoons olive oil
2 small onions, sliced
6 garlic cloves, thinly sliced
5 ounces chorizo sausage,
thickly sliced
14-ounce can chopped tomatoes
12–16 bay leaves
5 tablespoons medium sherry
salt and ground black pepper
rice or potatoes, to serve*

SERVES 4

1 | Preheat the oven to 375°F. Coat the chicken pieces in the paprika, making sure they are evenly covered, then season with salt. Heat the olive oil in a frying pan and sauté the chicken until brown.

2 | Transfer to an ovenproof dish. Add the onions to the pan and sauté quickly. Add the garlic and chorizo and sauté for 2 minutes.

3 | Add the tomatoes, two of the bay leaves and the sherry and bring to a boil. Pour over the chicken and cover with a lid. Bake for 45 minutes. Remove the lid and season to taste. Cook for another 20 minutes, until the chicken is tender and golden. Serve with rice or potatoes, garnished with bay leaves.

CHICKEN CASSEROLE WITH SPICED FIGS

The Spanish Catalans have various recipes for fruit with meat. This is quite an unusual one, but it uses one of the fruits most strongly associated with the Mediterranean—the fig.

FOR THE FIGS
⅔ cup sugar
½ cup white wine vinegar
1 lemon slice
1 cinnamon stick
1 pound fresh figs

FOR THE CHICKEN
½ cup medium-sweet white wine
pared zest of ½ lemon
3½-pound chicken, cut into
eight pieces
2 ounces lardons, or thick bacon
cut into strips
1 tablespoon olive oil
¼ cup chicken stock
salt and ground black pepper

SERVES 4

1 Put the sugar, vinegar, lemon slice and cinnamon stick in a pan with ½ cup water. Bring to a boil, then simmer for 5 minutes. Add the figs, cover, and simmer for 10 minutes. Remove from heat, cover, and let sit for 3 hours.

2 Preheat the oven to 350°F. Drain the figs and place in a bowl. Add the wine and lemon zest. Season the chicken. In a large frying pan, cook the lardons or bacon strips until the fat melts and they turn golden. Transfer to a shallow ovenproof dish, leaving any fat in the pan. Add the oil to the pan and brown the chicken pieces all over.

3 Drain the figs, adding the wine to the pan with the chicken. Boil until the sauce has reduced and is syrupy. Transfer the contents of the frying pan to the ovenproof dish and bake, uncovered, for about 20 minutes. Add the figs and chicken stock, cover and return to the oven for another 10 minutes. Serve with a green salad.

CHICKEN AND APRICOT PHYLLO PIE

The filling for this pie has a Middle Eastern flavor—chopped chicken combined with apricots, bulgur, nuts and spices.

½ cup bulgur
6 tablespoons butter
1 onion, chopped
1 pound chopped chicken
¼ cup dried apricots, finely chopped
¼ cup blanched almonds, chopped
1 teaspoon ground cinnamon
½ teaspoon ground allspice
¼ cup strained plain yogurt
1 tablespoon snipped fresh chives
2 tablespoons chopped fresh parsley
6 large sheets phyllo pastry
salt and ground black pepper
chives, to garnish

SERVES 6

1 Preheat the oven to 400°F. Put the bulgur in a bowl with ½ cup boiling water. Soak for 5–10 minutes, until the water is absorbed.

2 Heat 2 tablespoons of the butter in a pan and gently sauté the onion and chicken until pale golden.

3 Stir in the apricots, almonds and bulgur and cook for 2 more minutes. Remove from heat and stir in the cinnamon, allspice, yogurt, chives and parsley. Season to taste with salt and pepper.

4 Melt the remaining butter. Unroll the phyllo pastry and cut into 10-inch circles. Keep the pastry circles covered with a clean, damp dish towel to prevent drying.

5 Line a 9-inch quiche pan with a removable bottom with three of the pastry circles, brushing each one with butter as you layer them. Spoon in the chicken mixture and cover with three more pastry rounds, brushed with melted butter as before.

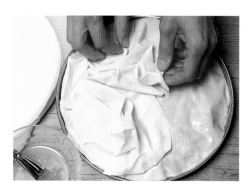

6 Crumple the remaining circles and place them on top of the pie, then brush on any remaining melted butter. Bake the pie for about 30 minutes, until the pastry is golden brown and crisp. Serve Chicken and Apricot Phyllo Pie hot or cold, cut into wedges and garnished with chives.

CASSOULET

Cassoulet is a classic French dish in which a feast of various meats is baked slowly with beans under a golden crumb crust. It is hearty and rich, perfect for a winter gathering.

3½ cups dried navy or
Great Northern beans
2 pounds salt pork or
pork pieces
4 large duck breasts
4 tablespoons olive oil
2 onions, chopped
6 garlic cloves, crushed
2 bay leaves
¼ teaspoon ground cloves
4 tablespoons tomato paste
8 good-quality sausages
4 tomatoes
1½ cups dried bread crumbs
salt and ground black pepper

SERVES 6–8

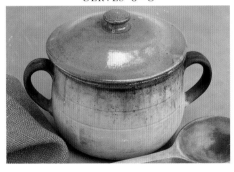

1 Put the beans in a large bowl and cover with plenty of cold water. Let soak overnight. If using salt pork, soak it overnight in water.

2 Drain the beans thoroughly and put them in a large saucepan with fresh water to cover. Bring to a boil and boil rapidly for 10 minutes. Drain and set the beans aside.

3 Cut the pork into large pieces, discarding the rind. Halve the duck breasts.

4 Heat 2 tablespoons of the oil in a frying pan and sauté the pork in batches until browned.

5 Put the beans in a large, heavy saucepan with the onions, garlic, bay leaves, ground cloves and tomato paste. Stir in the browned pork and just cover with water. Bring to a boil, then reduce the heat to the lowest setting and simmer, covered, for about 1½ hours, until the beans are tender.

6 Preheat the oven to 350°F. Heat the rest of the oil in a frying pan and sauté the duck breasts and sausages until browned. Cut the sausages into pieces.

7 Plunge the tomatoes into boiling water for 30 seconds, then refresh in cold water. Peel away the skins and cut them into quarters.

8 Transfer the bean mixture to a large earthenware pot or ovenproof dish and stir in the sausages, duck breasts and chopped tomatoes with salt and pepper to taste.

9 Sprinkle with an even layer of bread crumbs and bake for 45 minutes to 1 hour, until the crust is golden. Serve hot.

VARIATION
You can easily alter the proportions and types of meat and vegetables in a cassoulet. Turnips, carrots and celery root make suitable vegetable substitutes, while cubed lamb and goose can replace the pork and duck.

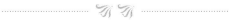

CHICKEN IN A SALT CRUST

Cooking food in a casing of salt gives a deliciously moist, tender flavor that, surprisingly, is not too salty. The technique is used in both Italy and France for chicken and whole fish, although chicken is easier to deal with.

4½-pound chicken
about 5 pounds coarse sea salt

FOR THE GARLIC PUREE
1 pound onions, quartered
2 large heads of garlic
½ cup olive oil
salt and ground black pepper

FOR THE ROASTED TOMATOES
AND PEPPERS
1 pound plum tomatoes
3 red bell peppers, seeded and
quartered
1 red chile, seeded and finely chopped
6 tablespoons olive oil
flat-leaf parsley, to garnish

SERVES 6

2 Truss the chicken tightly so that the salt cannot fall into the cavity. Sprinkle a thin layer of salt in the foil-lined dish, then place the chicken on top.

3 Pour the remaining salt all around and on the top of the chicken until it is completely encased. Sprinkle the top with a little water.

4 Cover tightly with the foil and bake the chicken on the lower oven shelf for 1¾ hours. Meanwhile, put the onions in a small, heavy saucepan. Break up the heads of garlic, but leave the skins on. Add to the pan with the olive oil and a little salt and pepper.

5 Cover and cook over the lowest possible heat for about 1 hour or until the garlic is completely soft.

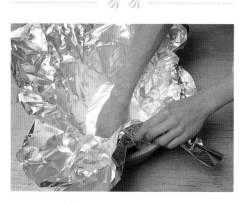

1 Preheat the oven to 425°F. Choose a deep ovenproof dish into which the whole chicken will fit snugly. Line the dish with a double layer of heavy foil, allowing plenty of excess foil to overhang the top edge of the ovenproof dish.

COOK'S TIP
This recipe makes a stunning main course when you want to serve something a little different. Take the salt-crusted chicken to the table garnished with plenty of fresh mixed herbs. Once you've scraped off the salt, transfer the chicken to a clean plate to carve it.

6 Plunge the tomatoes into boiling water for 30 seconds, then refresh in cold water. Peel off the skins and quarter the tomatoes. Put the red peppers, tomatoes and chile in a shallow ovenproof dish and sprinkle with the oil. Bake on the shelf above the chicken for 45 minutes, or until the peppers are slightly charred.

7 Squeeze the garlic out of the skins. Process the onions, garlic and pan juices in a blender or food processor until smooth. Return the purée to the clean saucepan.

8 To serve the chicken, open up the foil and ease it out of the dish. Place on a large serving platter. Transfer the roasted pepper mixture to a serving dish and garnish with parsley. Reheat the garlic purée. Crack open the salt crust on the chicken and brush off the salt before carving and serving with the garlic purée and pepper mixture.

SPICED DUCK WITH PEARS

This delicious casserole is based on a Catalan dish that uses goose or duck. The sautéed pears are added toward the end of cooking, along with picarda sauce, a pounded pine-nut and garlic paste that both flavors and thickens.

6 duck portions, either breast or
leg pieces
1 tablespoon olive oil
1 large onion, thinly sliced
1 cinnamon stick, halved
2 thyme sprigs
2 cups chicken stock

TO FINISH
3 firm, ripe pears
2 tablespoons olive oil
2 garlic cloves, sliced
⅓ cup pine nuts
½ teaspoon saffron strands
2 tablespoons raisins
salt and ground black pepper
young thyme sprigs or parsley,
to garnish

SERVES 6

1 Preheat the oven to 350°F. Sauté the duck portions in the olive oil for about 5 minutes, until the skin is golden. Transfer the duck to an ovenproof dish and drain off all but 1 tablespoon of the fat left in the pan.

2 Add the onion to the pan and sauté for 5 minutes. Add the cinnamon stick, thyme and stock and bring to a boil. Pour over the duck and bake for 1¼ hours.

3 Meanwhile, peel, core and halve the pears and sauté quickly in the oil until beginning to turn golden on the cut sides. Pound the garlic, pine nuts and saffron in a mortar with a pestle to make a thick, smooth paste.

4 Add the paste to the casserole along with the raisins and pears. Bake for another 15 minutes, until the pears are tender.

5 Season to taste with salt and pepper and garnish with parsley or thyme. Serve with mashed potatoes and a green vegetable, if desired.

COOK'S TIP
A good stock is essential for this dish. Buy a large duck (plus two extra duck breasts if you want portions to be generous) and cut it up yourself, using the giblets and carcass for stock. Alternatively, buy duck portions and canned chicken stock.

RABBIT SALMOREJO

Small pieces of rabbit, conveniently sold in packages at some supermarkets, make an interesting alternative to chicken in this light, spicy sauté from Spain. Serve with a simple dressed salad.

1½ pounds rabbit pieces
1¼ cups dry white wine
1 tablespoon sherry vinegar
several oregano sprigs
2 bay leaves
6 tablespoons olive oil
6 ounces baby onions, peeled and left whole
1 red chile, seeded and finely chopped
4 garlic cloves, sliced
2 teaspoons paprika
⅔ cup chicken stock
salt and ground black pepper
flat-leaf parsley sprigs, to garnish

SERVES 4

1 Put the rabbit in a bowl. Add the wine, vinegar, oregano and bay leaves and toss together lightly. Cover and let marinate for several hours or overnight.

2 Drain the rabbit, reserving the marinade, and pat dry on paper towels. Heat the oil in a large sauté or frying pan. Add the rabbit and sauté on all sides until golden, then remove with a slotted spoon. Sauté the onions until beginning to color.

3 Remove the onions from the pan and add the chile, garlic and paprika. Cook, stirring, for about a minute. Add the reserved marinade, with the stock. Season lightly.

4 Return the rabbit to the pan with the onions. Bring to a boil, then reduce the heat and cover with a lid. Simmer very gently for about 45 minutes, until the rabbit is tender. Serve garnished with a few sprigs of flat-leaf parsley, if desired.

COOK'S TIP
If more convenient, rather than cooking on top of the stove, transfer the stew to an ovenproof dish and bake at 350°F for about 50 minutes.

DUCK BREASTS WITH A WALNUT AND POMEGRANATE SAUCE

This is an extremely exotic sweet-and-sour dish that originally came from Persia.

4 tablespoons olive oil
2 onions, very thinly sliced
½ teaspoon ground turmeric
3½ cups walnuts, coarsely chopped
4 cups duck or chicken stock
6 pomegranates
2 tablespoons sugar
¼ cup lemon juice
4 duck breasts, about 8 ounces each
salt and ground black pepper

SERVES 6

COOK'S TIP
Choose pomegranates with shiny, brightly colored skins. The juice stains, so be careful when cutting them. Only the seeds are used in cooking; the pith is discarded.

1. Heat half the oil in a frying pan. Add the onions and turmeric and cook gently until soft. Transfer to a pan, add the walnuts and stock, then season with salt and pepper. Stir, then bring to a boil and simmer the mixture, uncovered, for 20 minutes.

2. Cut the pomegranates in half and scoop out the seeds into a bowl, reserving the seeds of one pomegranate. Transfer the remaining seeds to a blender or food processor and process to break them up. Put through a strainer to extract the juice and stir in the sugar and lemon juice.

3. Score the skin of the duck breasts in a lattice fashion with a sharp knife. Heat the remaining oil in a frying pan or grill pan and place the duck breasts in it, skin side down.

4. Cook gently for 10 minutes, pouring off the fat from time to time, until the skin is dark golden and crisp. Turn the duck breasts over and cook for another 3–4 minutes. Transfer to a plate and allow to rest.

5. Deglaze the frying pan or grill pan with the pomegranate juice mixture, stirring with a wooden spoon, then add the walnut and stock mixture and simmer for 15 minutes, until the sauce has thickened slightly. Serve the duck breasts sliced, drizzled with a little sauce, and garnished with the reserved pomegranate seeds. Serve the remaining sauce separately.

SQUAB BREASTS WITH PANCETTA

Mild, succulent squab breasts are easy to cook and make an impressive main course for a special dinner.
Serve this Italian-style dish with polenta and some simple green vegetables.

4 whole squabs
2 large onions
2 carrots, coarsely chopped
1 celery stalk, trimmed and
coarsely chopped
1 ounce dried porcini mushrooms
2 ounces pancetta
2 tablespoons butter
2 tablespoons olive oil
2 garlic cloves, crushed
⅔ cup red wine
salt and ground black pepper
flat-leaf parsley, to garnish
cooked oyster mushrooms, to serve

SERVES 4

2   Put the squab carcasses in a large saucepan. Halve one of the onions, leaving the skin on. Add to the pan with the carrots and celery and just cover with water. Bring to a boil, reduce the heat and simmer very gently, uncovered, for about 1½ hours, to make a dark, rich stock. Let cool slightly, then strain into a bowl.

3   Cover the porcini mushrooms with ⅔ cup hot water and let soak for at least 30 minutes. Chop the pancetta.

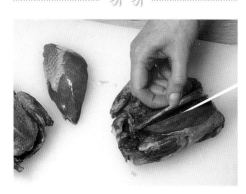

1   To prepare a squab, cut down the length of the bird just to one side of the breastbone. Gradually scrape off the meat from the breastbone until the breast comes away completely. Do the same on the other side, then repeat with the remaining squabs.

4   Peel and finely chop the remaining onion. Melt half the butter with the oil in a large frying pan. Add the onion and pancetta and sauté very gently for 3 minutes. Add the squab breasts, skin side down, and sauté for 2 minutes, until browned. Turn over and sauté for another 2 minutes.

5   Add the mushrooms with their soaking liquid, garlic, wine and 1 cup of the stock. Bring just to a boil, then reduce the heat and simmer gently for 5 minutes, until the squab breasts are tender but still a little pink in the center.

6   Lift out the squab breasts and keep them hot. Return the sauce to a boil and boil rapidly to reduce slightly. Gradually whisk in all the remaining butter and season with salt and pepper to taste.

7   Transfer the squab breasts to warmed serving plates and pour on the sauce. Serve immediately, garnished with sprigs of parsley and accompanied by oyster mushrooms.

COOK'S TIP
If buying squab from a butcher, order them in advance and ask him to remove the breasts for you. You can also cut off the legs and sauté these with the breasts, although there is little meat on them and you might prefer to let them flavor the stock.

MOROCCAN PIGEON PIE

This recipe is based upon a classic Moroccan dish called Pastilla, which is a phyllo pastry pie filled with an unusual but delicious mixture of squab, eggs, spices and nuts. If squab is unavailable, chicken makes a good substitute.

3 squabs
4 tablespoons butter
1 onion, chopped
1 cinnamon stick
½ teaspoon ground ginger
2 tablespoons chopped fresh cilantro
3 tablespoons chopped parsley
pinch of ground turmeric
1 tablespoon sugar
¼ teaspoon ground cinnamon
1 cup toasted almonds, finely chopped
6 eggs, beaten
salt and ground black pepper
cinnamon and confectioners' sugar,
to garnish

FOR THE PASTRY
12 tablespoons (1½ sticks) butter,
melted
16 sheets phyllo pastry
1 egg yolk

SERVES 6

1. Wash the squabs and place in a pan with the butter, onion, cinnamon stick, ginger, cilantro, parsley and turmeric. Season with salt and pepper. Add just enough water to cover and bring to a boil. Cover and simmer gently for about 1 hour, until the squab is very tender.

2. Strain off the stock and reserve. Skin and bone the squabs, and shred the flesh into bite-size pieces. Preheat the oven to 350°F. Combine the sugar, cinnamon and almonds, and set aside.

3. Measure ⅔ cup of the reserved stock into a small pan. Add the eggs and mix well. Stir over low heat until creamy and very thick and almost set. Season with salt and pepper.

4. Brush a 12-inch diameter ovenproof dish with some of the melted butter and lay the first sheet of pastry in the dish. Brush this with butter and continue with five more sheets of pastry. Cover with the almond mixture, then half the egg mixture. Moisten with a little stock.

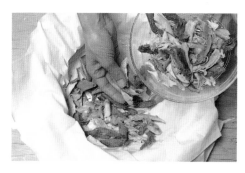

5. Layer four more sheets of phyllo pastry, brushing with butter as before. Lay the squab meat on top. Add the remaining egg mixture and more stock. Cover with the remaining pastry, brushing each sheet with butter, and tuck in any overlapping edges.

6. Brush the pie with egg yolk and bake for 40 minutes. Raise the oven temperature to 400°F and bake for 15 minutes more, until the pastry is crisp and golden. Garnish with a lattice design of cinnamon and confectioners' sugar. Serve hot.

GRAINS AND BEANS

Mediterranean countries deserve thanks for the
creation of risotto, paella, pizzas and pasta, and the
many salads and stews based on dried peas and beans.

The countries surrounding the Mediterranean produce a seemingly inexhaustible quantity and variety of grains, peas and beans. Wheat, the most ancient cereal grown in the region, predominates. It is the staple that provides for traditional and specialized local dishes, but from centuries of trading and travel come a great number of dishes that, although originally associated with one country, are often made using slightly different techniques and ingredients in many different areas of the Mediterranean.

Pasta, for example, although most widely consumed in Italy, is also made in the eastern Mediterranean under the name of **rishta**; it is known in Spain as **fideos**, and in Egypt as **macaroni or koshari**.

Bread is a staple food all over the Mediterranean. When you consider that it is made using the same basic ingredients, it is remarkable that there is such a variety of flavors and textures. There are the Italian olive breads—focaccia and ciabatta—and the dry breads like grissini and crostini, as well as a feast of soft breads, richly flavored with sun-dried tomatoes and herbs. Visit

BELOW: Spain produces a wide range of grains of all types, seen here at a typical market.

any part of France and see how important freshly baked breads, from rich brioches to crisp baguettes, are to the French. Bakeries stay open all through the day, turning out batch after batch of hot loaves. French bakers do not depend on preservatives, so bread has to be prepared fresh for every meal. Festive breads are also still widely enjoyed. The most elaborate is the braided Greek Easter Bread, flavored with nuts and fruit and adorned with hard-boiled eggs that are dyed red. According to legend, the eggs will keep those who eat them safe from harm.

The unleavened or slightly leavened flat breads of the eastern Mediterranean and North Africa are eaten with every meal. The most common of these is the pita, which varies in shape and size. The Turks bake a huge, flat loaf that inflates like a balloon during baking. This is carried ceremoniously to the table, where it is shared by the diners; its soft, chewy dough is perfect for mopping up spicy sauces. Pita bread is often used instead of knives and forks; when slit, the empty pocket makes a perfect container for salads, bean dishes, falafel and meats.

Wheat flour is also used to make the highly popular phyllo pastries of North Africa, Lebanon, Greece and Turkey. It is skillfully shaped and stretched to form a transparent sheet, which is then brushed with olive oil or melted butter and folded into layers. When cooked, it is extremely flaky, light and crisp. Phyllo is used in many sweet or savory classics, such as the Moroccan pastilla, a spicy squab pie with cloves and cinnamon.

Regional classics like North African couscous are also made with wheat. Couscous is a kind of wheat pasta that gives its name to the traditional dish of either a spiced meat or vegetable sauce that covers the steamed pasta. At its most splendid it is served as a finale to a special feast when guests have already enjoyed several delicate courses. The couscous is piled high on a large platter and topped with meat or vegetables smothered in a delectable sweet, spicy sauce.

ABOVE: The fertile Guadalquivir valley near Carmona, in Spain.

Rice has been central to Mediterranean cooking for as long as twelve thousand years. The Moors brought rice to Europe in the eighth century through the eastern Mediterranean from Persia and Asia. With its strong Moorish tradition, southern Spain, particularly Valencia, remains the country's main producer of rice. The national dish, paella, originated in the coastal cities and fishing ports of Andalusia. But the uses for rice extend much further than one national dish. Many other rich, saffron-flavored risottos are widely popular and are good with zarzuela, an extravagant feast of fish and crustacea. Italians also consume a lot of rice, predominantly arborio, a short-grain, starchy rice that cooks down to a soft, creamy consistency. Arborio supplies the authentic taste of the classic subtle accompaniment Risotto alla Milanese, which is enriched with saffron, wine and Parmesan. In contrast, the fiery, dry pilafs of Turkey and the Middle East are heavily spiced and mixed with numerous herbs, dried fruits, nuts and vegetables.

Chickpeas are perhaps the most popular of the Mediterranean peas and form the basis of creamy pastes like hummus. Along with other peas and beans they are widely used in cold, garlicky dressed salads and as the base of many soups.

Traditionally a peasant food, beans are given long, slow cooking, and their taste is enhanced with cheap but flavorful meats or garlic-cured sausages. Served with locally produced vegetables, beans are the heart of many delicious soups and stews—for example, the traditional cassoulet of France. Before cooking dried beans, soak them in water overnight. Drain, cover with fresh water, then boil them rapidly for ten minutes to eliminate the sugars that cause indigestion. Reduce the heat and simmer for the rest of the recommended cooking time. Only add salt toward the end of the cooking time—if added too soon, salt will toughen the beans.

199

HUMMUS BI TAHINA

Blending chickpeas with garlic and oil makes a surprisingly creamy purée that is delicious as part of a Turkish-style mezze, or as a dip with vegetables. Leftovers make good sandwiches.

¾ cup dried chickpeas
juice of 2 lemons
2 garlic cloves, sliced
2 tablespoons olive oil
pinch of cayenne pepper
⅔ cup tahini paste
salt and ground black pepper
extra olive oil and cayenne pepper
for sprinkling
flat-leaf parsley, to garnish

SERVES 4–6

1 Put the chickpeas in a bowl with plenty of cold water and let soak overnight.

2 Drain the chickpeas and cover with fresh water in a saucepan. Bring to a boil and boil rapidly for 10 minutes. Reduce the heat and simmer gently for about 1 hour, until soft. Drain.

3 Process the chickpeas in a food processor to a smooth purée. Add the lemon juice, garlic, olive oil, cayenne pepper and tahini and blend until creamy, scraping the mixture down from the sides of the bowl.

4 Season the purée with salt and pepper and transfer to a serving dish. Sprinkle with oil and cayenne pepper and serve garnished with a few parsley sprigs.

COOK'S TIP
For convenience, canned chickpeas can be used instead of dried. Use two 14-ounce cans and drain them thoroughly. Tahini paste can now be purchased at most supermarkets or health-food stores.

FALAFEL

In North Africa, these spicy fritters are made using dried fava beans, but chickpeas are much easier to find. Falafel are great served as a snack with garlicky yogurt or stuffed into warmed pita bread.

¾ cup dried chickpeas
1 large onion, coarsely chopped
2 garlic cloves, coarsely chopped
4 tablespoons coarsely chopped parsley
1 teaspoon cumin seeds, crushed
1 teaspoon coriander seeds, crushed
½ teaspoon baking powder
salt and ground black pepper
oil for deep-frying
pita bread, salad and yogurt,
to serve

SERVES 4

1 Put the chickpeas in a bowl with plenty of cold water. Let soak overnight.

2 Drain the chickpeas and cover with water in a pan. Bring to a boil. Boil rapidly for 10 minutes. Reduce the heat and simmer for about 1 hour, until soft. Drain.

3 Place in a food processor with the onion, garlic, parsley, cumin, coriander and baking powder. Add salt and pepper to taste. Process until the mixture forms a firm paste.

4 Shape the mixture into walnut-size balls and flatten them slightly. In a deep pan, heat 2 inches oil until a little of the mixture sizzles on the surface when added. Fry the falafel in batches until golden. Drain on paper towels and keep hot while frying the remainder. Serve warm, in pita bread, with salad and yogurt.

SUN-DRIED TOMATO BREAD

In the south of Italy, tomatoes are often dried in the hot sun. They are then preserved in oil, or hung up on strings in the kitchen, to use in the winter. This recipe uses the former type.

6 cups all-purpose flour
2 teaspoons salt
2 tablespoons sugar
1 package active dry yeast
1⅔–2 cups warm milk
1 tablespoon tomato paste
5 tablespoons oil from the jar of sun-dried tomatoes
5 tablespoons extra virgin olive oil
¾ cup drained sun-dried tomatoes, chopped
1 large onion, chopped

MAKES 4 SMALL LOAVES

2 Mix the tomato paste into the remaining milk until evenly blended, then add to the flour with the tomato oil and olive oil.

4 Punch down, and add the tomatoes and onion. Knead until evenly distributed through the dough. Shape into four loaves and place on a greased baking sheet. Cover with a dish towel and let rise again for about 45 minutes.

5 Preheat the oven to 375°F. Bake the bread for 45 minutes or until the loaves sound hollow when you tap them with your fingers. Let cool on a wire rack. Eat warm, or toasted with grated mozzarella cheese sprinkled on top.

3 Gradually mix the flour into the liquid ingredients until you have a dough. Turn out onto a floured surface and knead for about 10 minutes, until smooth and elastic. Return to the clean bowl, cover with a cloth and let rise in a warm place for about 2 hours.

1 Sift the flour, salt and sugar into a bowl, and make a well in the center. Mix the yeast with ⅔ cup of the warm milk and add to the flour.

COOK'S TIP
Use a pair of sharp kitchen scissors to cut up the sun-dried tomatoes.

GREEK EASTER BREAD

In Greece, Easter celebrations are very important and involve much preparation in the kitchen. This bread is sold in all the bakers' shops and also made at home. It is traditionally decorated with eggs dyed red.

1 package active dry yeast
½ cup warm milk
6 cups bread flour
2 eggs, beaten
½ teaspoon caraway seeds
1 tablespoon sugar
1 tablespoon brandy
4 tablespoons butter, melted
1 egg white, beaten
2–3 hard-boiled eggs, dyed red
½ cup split almonds

MAKES 1 LOAF

1 Mix the yeast with one or two tablespoons of warm water and set aside until it bubbles. Add the milk and 1 cup of the flour and mix to a creamy consistency. Cover with a cloth and let rest in a warm place to rise for 1 hour.

COOK'S TIP
For a nontraditional but festive variation, dye the eggs in different, spring-like colors.

2 Sift the remaining flour into a large bowl and make a well in the center. Pour the risen yeast mixture into the well and draw in a little of the flour from the sides. Add the eggs, caraway seeds, sugar and brandy. Incorporate the remaining flour until the mixture begins to form a dough.

3 Mix in the melted butter. Turn out onto a floured surface and knead for about 10 minutes, until the dough becomes smooth. Return to the bowl and cover with a cloth. Let rise in a warm place for 3 hours.

4 Preheat the oven to 350°F. Punch down the dough, turn out onto a floured surface and knead for a minute or two. Divide the dough into three pieces and roll each piece into a long sausage. Make a braid, as shown above, and place the loaf on a greased baking sheet.

5 Tuck the ends under, brush with the egg white and decorate with the eggs and split almonds. Bake for about 1 hour, until the loaf sounds hollow when tapped on the bottom. Cool on a wire rack.

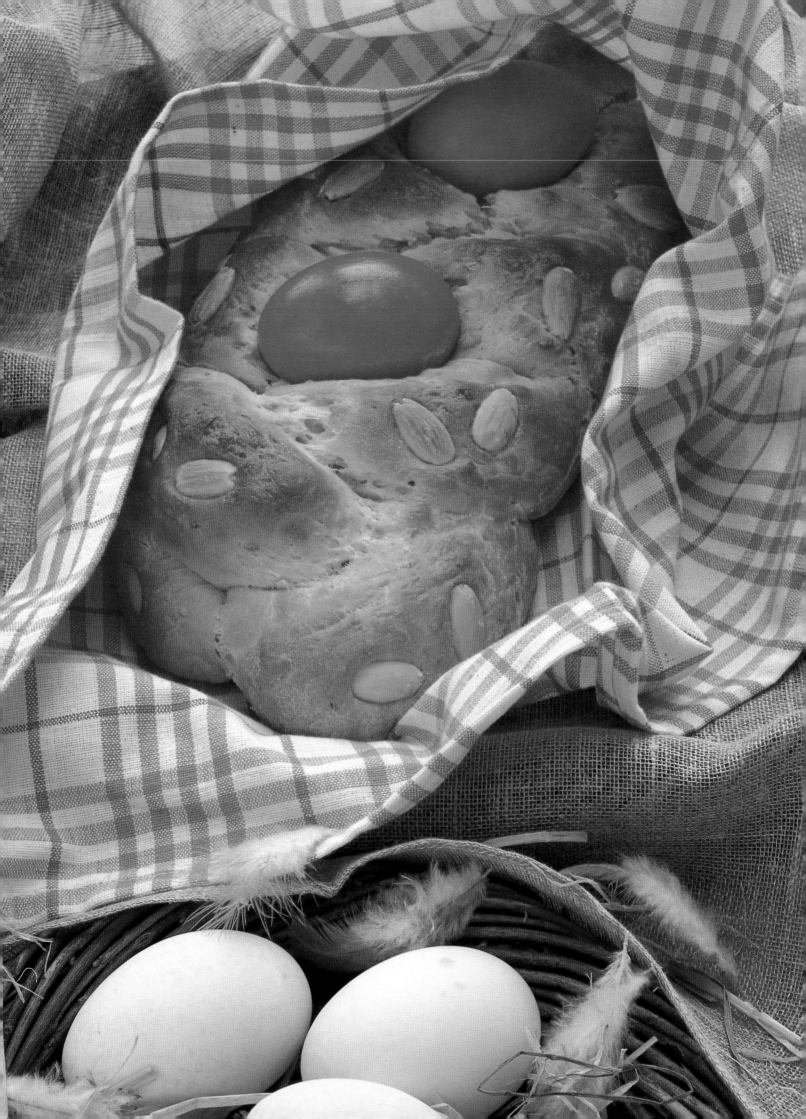

FOCACCIA

This is a flattish bread, originating in Genoa, Italy, made with flour, olive oil and salt. There are many variations from many regions, including stuffed varieties and versions topped with onions, olives or herbs.

1 package active dry yeast
3½ cups all-purpose flour
2 teaspoons salt
5 tablespoons olive oil
2 teaspoons coarse sea salt

MAKES 1 ROUND 10-INCH LOAF

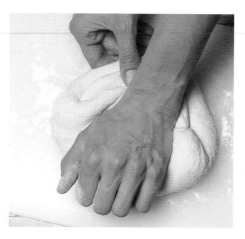

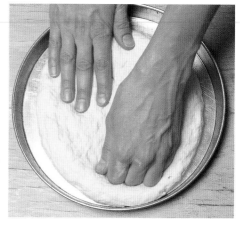

1 Dissolve the yeast in ½ cup warm water. Let stand for 10 minutes. Sift the flour into a large bowl, make a well in the center, and add the yeast mixture, salt and 2 tablespoons oil. Mix in the flour and add more water to make a dough.

2 Turn out onto a floured surface and knead the dough for about 10 minutes, until smooth and elastic. Return to the bowl, cover with a cloth, and let rise in a warm place for 2–2½ hours, until the dough has doubled in bulk.

3 Punch down the dough and knead again for a few minutes. Press into an oiled 10-inch tart pan and cover with a damp cloth. Let rise for 30 minutes.

4 Preheat the oven to 400°F. Poke the dough all over with your fingers to make little dimples in the surface. Pour the remaining oil over the dough, using a pastry brush to take it to the edges. Sprinkle with the salt.

5 Bake for 20–25 minutes, until the bread is pale gold. Carefully remove from the pan and let cool on a rack. The bread is best eaten on the same day, but it also freezes very well.

ONION FOCACCIA

This pizza-like flat bread is characterized by its soft, dimpled surface, sometimes dredged simply with coarse salt or with onions, herbs or olives. It tastes delicious served warm with soups and stews.

6 cups all-purpose flour
½ teaspoon salt
½ teaspoon sugar
1 tablespoon rapid-rise yeast
4 tablespoons extra virgin olive oil
2 cups warm water

TO FINISH
2 red onions, thinly sliced
3 tablespoons extra virgin olive oil
1 tablespoon coarse salt

MAKES TWO 10-INCH BREADS

1. Sift the flour, salt and sugar into a large bowl. Stir in the yeast, oil and water and mix to a dough using a round-bladed knife. (Add a little extra water if the dough is dry.)

2. Turn out onto a lightly floured surface and knead for about 10 minutes, until smooth and elastic.

3. Put the dough in a clean, lightly oiled bowl and cover with plastic wrap. Let rise in a warm place until doubled in bulk.

4. Place two 10-inch plain metal baking rings on baking sheets. Oil the insides of the rings and the baking sheets.

5. Preheat the oven to 400°F. Halve the dough and roll out each piece to a 10-inch circle. Press into the rings, cover with a dampened dish towel and let rise for 30 minutes.

6. Make deep holes, about 1 inch apart, in the dough. Cover and let rest for another 20 minutes.

7. Sprinkle the onions on top and drizzle with the oil. Sprinkle with the salt, then a little cold water, to prevent a crust from forming.

8. Bake for about 25 minutes, sprinkling with water again during cooking. Cool on a wire rack.

PAPPARDELLE WITH OLIVE AND CAPER PASTE

This homemade pasta is flavored with sun-dried tomato paste. The results are well worth the effort, but store-bought pasta can be substituted for a quick supper dish.

FOR THE PASTA
2½ cups all-purpose flour
¼ teaspoon salt
3 eggs
3 tablespoons sun-dried tomato paste

FOR THE SAUCE
⅔ cup pitted black olives
5 tablespoons capers
5 drained anchovy fillets
1 red chile, seeded and
coarsely chopped
¼ cup coarsely chopped basil
¼ cup coarsely chopped parsley
⅔ cup olive oil
4 ripe tomatoes
salt and ground black pepper
flat leaf parsley or basil, to garnish
Parmesan cheese shavings, to serve

SERVES 4

1 To make the pasta, sift the flour and salt into a bowl and make a well in the center. Lightly beat the eggs with the tomato paste and pour the mixture into the well.

2 Combine the ingredients using a round-bladed knife. Turn out onto a work surface and knead for 6–8 minutes, until the dough is very smooth and soft, working in a little more flour if it becomes sticky. Wrap in aluminum foil and chill for 30 minutes.

3 To make the sauce, put the olives, capers, anchovies, chile, basil and parsley in a food processor or blender with the oil. Process very briefly until the ingredients are finely chopped. (Alternatively, you can finely chop the ingredients and then mix with the olive oil.)

4 Plunge the tomatoes into boiling water for 30 seconds, then refresh in cold water. Peel away the skins, remove the seeds and dice. Roll out the dough very thinly on a floured surface. Sprinkle with a little flour, then roll up like a jelly roll. Cut crosswise into ½-inch slices.

5 Unroll the pasta and lay out on a clean dish towel for about 10 minutes to dry.

6 Bring a large saucepan of salted water to a boil. Add the pasta and cook for 2–3 minutes, until just tender. Drain immediately and return to the saucepan.

7 Add the olive mixture, tomatoes and salt and black pepper to taste, then toss together gently over medium heat for about 1 minute, until heated through. Garnish with parsley or basil and serve sprinkled with Parmesan shavings.

SPANISH ONION AND ANCHOVY PIZZA

This pizza has flavors and ingredients brought to Spain by the Moors and still used today in many classic Spanish recipes.

2½ cups all-purpose flour
½ teaspoon salt
½ ounce rapid-rise yeast
½ cup olive oil
⅔ cup milk and water, in equal
quantities, combined
3 large onions, thinly sliced
2-ounce can anchovies, drained and
coarsely chopped
2 tablespoons pine nuts
2 tablespoons golden raisins
1 teaspoon red pepper flakes
salt and ground black pepper

SERVES 6–8

1 Sift the flour and salt together into a large bowl. Stir in the yeast. Make a well in the center, and add half of the olive oil and a little of the milk and water. Bring the flour mixture and liquid together, gradually adding the remaining milk and water, until a dough is formed. Knead on a floured surface for about 10 minutes. Return to the bowl, cover with a cloth, and set in a warm place to rise for about 1 hour.

2 Heat the remaining oil in a large frying pan, add the onions and cook until soft. Preheat the oven to 475°F.

3 Punch down the dough and roll out to a rectangle about 12 x 15 inches. Place on an oiled baking sheet. Cover with the onions. Sprinkle on the anchovies, pine nuts, golden raisins and red pepper flakes. Season. Bake for 10–15 minutes, until the edges are beginning to brown. Serve hot.

MUSHROOM AND PESTO PIZZA

Home-made Italian-style pizzas are a little time-consuming to make, but the results are well worth the effort.

FOR THE PIZZA CRUST
3 cups all-purpose flour
¼ teaspoon salt
½ ounce rapid-rise yeast
1 tablespoon olive oil

FOR THE FILLING
2 ounces dried porcini mushrooms
¾ cup fresh basil
⅓ cup pine nuts
1½ ounces Parmesan cheese,
thinly sliced
7 tablespoons olive oil
2 onions, thinly sliced
8 ounces cremini mushrooms, sliced
salt and ground black pepper

SERVES 4

1 To make the pizza crust, put the flour in a bowl with the salt, yeast and olive oil. Add 1 cup warm water and mix to a dough using a round-bladed knife.

2 Turn out onto a work surface and knead for 5 minutes, until smooth. Place in a clean bowl, cover with plastic wrap and let rise in a warm place until doubled in bulk.

3 Meanwhile, make the filling. Soak the dried mushrooms in hot water for 20 minutes. Place the basil, pine nuts, Parmesan and 5 tablespoons of the olive oil in a blender or food processor and process to make a smooth paste. Set the paste aside.

4 Fry the onions in the remaining olive oil for 3–4 minutes, until beginning to color. Add the cremini mushrooms and fry for 2 minutes. Stir in the drained porcini mushrooms and season lightly.

5 Preheat the oven to 425°F. Lightly grease a large baking sheet. Turn out the pizza dough onto a floured surface and roll out to a 12-inch circle. Place the dough on the baking sheet.

6 Spread the pesto mixture to within ½ inch of the edges. Spread the mushroom mixture on top.

7 Bake the pizza for 35–40 minutes, until risen and golden.

OLIVE BREAD

Olive breads are popular all over the Mediterranean. For this Greek recipe use rich, oily olives or those marinated in herbs rather than canned ones.

2 red onions, thinly sliced
2 tablespoons olive oil
1⅓ cups pitted black or green olives
7 cups all-purpose flour
1½ teaspoons salt
4 teaspoons rapid-rise yeast
3 tablespoons each coarsely-chopped
parsley and cilantro or mint

MAKES TWO 1½-POUND LOAVES

1 | Sauté the onions in the oil until soft. Coarsely chop the olives.

2 | Put the flour, salt, yeast, parsley and cilantro or mint in a large bowl with the olives and onions and pour in 2 cups warm water.

VARIATION

Shape the dough into 16 small rolls. Slash the tops as above and reduce the cooking time to 25 minutes.

3 | Mix to a dough using a round-bladed knife, adding a little more water if the mixture feels dry.

4 | Turn out onto a lightly floured surface and knead for about 10 minutes. Put in a clean bowl, cover with plastic wrap and let sit in a warm place until doubled in bulk.

5 | Preheat the oven to 425°F. Lightly grease two baking sheets. Turn the dough out onto a floured surface and cut in half. Shape into two loaves and place on the baking sheets. Cover loosely with lightly oiled plastic wrap and let rise until doubled in size.

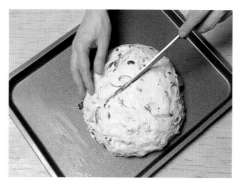

6 | Slash the tops of the loaves with a knife, then bake for about 40 minutes or until the loaves sound hollow when tapped on the bottom. Transfer to a wire rack to cool.

STUFFED KIBBEH

Kibbeh is a tasty North African specialty of ground meat and bulgur. The patties are sometimes stuffed with additional meat and deep-fried. Moderately spiced, they're good with yogurt or cacik sauce.

1 pound lean lamb (or lean ground
lamb or beef)
oil for deep-frying
avocado slices and cilantro sprigs,
to serve

FOR THE KIBBEH
1⅓ cups bulgur
1 red chile, seeded and
coarsely chopped
1 onion, coarsely chopped
salt and ground black pepper

FOR THE STUFFING
1 onion, finely chopped
⅔ cup pine nuts
2 tablespoons olive oil
1½ teaspoons ground allspice
¼ cup chopped cilantro

SERVES 4–6

1 If necessary, coarsely cut up the lamb and process the pieces in a blender or food processor until ground. Divide the ground meat into two equal portions.

2 To make the kibbeh, soak the bulgur for 15 minutes in cold water. Drain well, then process in the blender or food processor with the chile, onion, half the meat and plenty of salt and pepper.

3 To make the stuffing, fry the onion and pine nuts in the oil for 5 minutes. Add the allspice and remaining ground meat and fry gently, breaking up the meat with a wooden spoon, until browned. Stir in the cilantro and a little seasoning.

4 Turn the kibbeh mixture out onto a work surface and shape into a cake. Cut into 12 wedges.

5 Flatten one piece in the palm of your hand and spoon a little stuffing into the center. Bring the edges of the kibbeh up over the stuffing to enclose it. Make into a firm, egg-shaped mold between the palms of your hands, making sure that the filling is completely encased. Repeat with the other kibbeh.

6 Heat oil to a depth of 2 inches in a large pan, until a few kibbeh crumbs sizzle on the surface.

7 Lower half the kibbeh into the oil and fry for about 5 minutes, until golden. Drain on paper towels and keep them hot while cooking the remainder. Serve with avocado slices and cilantro sprigs.

EGYPTIAN RICE WITH LENTILS

Lentils are cooked with spices in many ways in the Middle East. Two important staples come together in this dish, which can be served hot or cold.

1½ cups large brown lentils, soaked
overnight in water
2 large onions
3 tablespoons olive oil
1 tablespoon ground cumin
½ teaspoon ground cinnamon
generous 1 cup long-grain rice
salt and ground black pepper
flat-leaf parsley, to garnish

SERVES 6

 Drain the lentils and put in a large pan. Add enough water to cover by 2 inches. Bring to a boil, cover the pan and simmer for 40 minutes to 1½ hours or until tender. Drain thoroughly.

2 Finely chop one onion and slice the other. Heat 1 tablespoon oil in a pan, add the chopped onion and sauté until soft. Add the lentils, salt, pepper, cumin and cinnamon.

3 Measure out the rice and add it, with the same volume of water, to the lentil mixture. Cover and simmer for about 20 minutes, until both the rice and lentils are tender. Heat the remaining oil in a frying pan and cook the sliced onion until very dark brown. Pour the rice mixture into a serving bowl, sprinkle with the onion and serve hot or cold, garnished with flat-leaf parsley.

BAKED CHEESE POLENTA WITH TOMATO SAUCE

Polenta, or cornmeal mush, is a staple food in Italy. It is cooked like a sort of porridge, and eaten soft, or set, cut into shapes, then baked or broiled.

1 teaspoon salt
2¼ cups instant polenta
1 teaspoon paprika
½ teaspoon ground nutmeg
2 tablespoons olive oil
1 large onion, finely chopped
2 garlic cloves, crushed
2 14-ounce cans chopped tomatoes
1 tablespoon tomato paste
1 teaspoon sugar
salt and ground black pepper
3 ounces Gruyère cheese, grated

SERVES 4

1 Preheat the oven to 400°F. Line an 11 x 7-inch baking pan with plastic wrap. Put 4 cups water into a pan and bring to a boil with the salt.

2 Pour in the polenta in a steady stream and cook, stirring constantly, for 5 minutes. Beat in the paprika and nutmeg, then pour into the prepared pan and smooth the surface. Let cool.

3 Heat the oil in a pan and cook the onion and garlic until soft. Add the tomatoes, paste and sugar. Season. Simmer for 20 minutes.

4 Turn out the polenta onto a cutting board and cut into 2-inch squares. Place half the squares in a greased ovenproof dish. Spoon on half the tomato sauce, and sprinkle with half the cheese. Repeat the layers. Bake for about 25 minutes, until golden.

PILAF WITH SAFFRON AND PICKLED WALNUTS

Pickled walnuts have a warm, tangy flavor that is delicious in rice and bulgur dishes. This eastern Mediterranean pilaf is interesting enough to serve on its own or with broiled lamb or pork.

1 teaspoon saffron strands
½ cup pine nuts
3 tablespoons olive oil
1 large onion, chopped
3 garlic cloves, crushed
¼ teaspoon ground allspice
1½-inch piece fresh ginger, grated
generous 1 cup long-grain rice
1¼ cups vegetable stock
½ cup pickled walnuts, drained and
coarsely chopped
¼ cup raisins
3 tablespoons coarsely chopped parsley
or cilantro
salt and ground black pepper
parsley or cilantro, to garnish
plain yogurt, to serve

SERVES 4

1 Put the saffron in a bowl with 1 tablespoon boiling water and let stand. Heat a large frying pan and dry-fry the pine nuts until they turn golden. Set them aside.

2 Heat the oil in the pan and sauté the onion, garlic and allspice for 3 minutes. Stir in the ginger and rice and cook for 1 more minute.

3 Add the stock and bring to a boil. Reduce the heat, cover and simmer gently for 15 minutes, until the rice is just tender.

4 Stir in the saffron and liquid, the pine nuts, pickled walnuts, raisins and parsley or cilantro. Season to taste with salt and pepper. Heat through gently for 2 minutes. Garnish with parsley or cilantro leaves and serve with plain yogurt.

VARIATION
Use one small eggplant, chopped and sautéed in a little olive oil, instead of the pickled walnuts, if you prefer.

RISOTTO ALLA MILANESE

—

Italian risottos have a distinctive creamy texture that is achieved using arborio rice, a short-grain rice that absorbs plenty of stock but at the same time retains some texture. This risotto, sprinkled with cheese and gremolata, makes a delicious light meal or accompaniment to a meaty stew or casserole.

FOR THE GREMOLATA
2 garlic cloves, crushed
¼ cup chopped fresh parsley
finely grated zest of 1 lemon

FOR THE RISOTTO
1 teaspoon saffron strands
2 tablespoons butter
1 large onion, finely chopped
1½ cups arborio (risotto) rice
⅔ cup dry white wine
4 cups chicken or
vegetable stock
salt and ground black pepper
Parmesan cheese shavings

SERVES 4

1　To make the gremolata, combine the garlic, parsley and lemon zest and reserve.

2　To make the risotto, put the saffron in a small bowl with 1 tablespoon boiling water and set aside. Melt the butter in a heavy saucepan and gently sauté the onion for 5 minutes.

3　Stir in the rice and cook for about 2 minutes, until it becomes translucent. Add the wine and saffron mixture and cook for several minutes, until the wine is absorbed.

4　Add 2½ cups of the stock to the pan and simmer gently until the stock is absorbed, stirring frequently.

5　Gradually add more stock, a ladleful at a time, until the rice is tender. (The rice might be tender and creamy before you've added all the stock, so add it slowly toward the end of the cooking time.)

6　Season the risotto with salt and pepper and transfer to a serving dish. Sprinkle lavishly with shavings of Parmesan cheese and the gremolata.

VARIATION
If preferred, stir plenty of grated Parmesan cheese into the risotto.

SPICED VEGETABLE COUSCOUS

Couscous, a cereal processed from semolina, is used throughout North Africa, mostly in Morocco, where it is served with meat, poultry and vegetable stews or tagines.

3 tablespoons vegetable oil
1 large onion, finely chopped
2 garlic cloves, crushed
1 tablespoon tomato paste
½ teaspoon ground turmeric
½ teaspoon cayenne pepper
1 teaspoon ground coriander
1 teaspoon ground cumin
1½ cups cauliflower florets
8 ounces baby carrots, trimmed
1 red bell pepper, seeded and diced
4 beefsteak tomatoes
8 ounces zucchini, thickly sliced
14-ounce can chickpeas, drained
and rinsed
3 tablespoons chopped cilantro
salt and ground black pepper
cilantro sprigs, to garnish

FOR THE COUSCOUS
1 teaspoon salt
2⅔ cups couscous
2 tablespoons butter

SERVES 6

 Heat 2 tablespoons of the oil in a large pan, add the onion and garlic, and cook until soft. Stir in the tomato paste, turmeric, cayenne, ground coriander and cumin. Cook, stirring, for 2 minutes.

 Add the cauliflower, carrots and pepper, with enough water to come halfway up the vegetables. Bring to a boil, then lower the heat, cover and simmer for 10 minutes.

COOK'S TIP
Beefsteak tomatoes have excellent flavor and are ideal for this recipe, but you can substitute six ordinary tomatoes or two 14-ounce cans chopped tomatoes.

 Plunge the tomatoes into boiling water for 30 seconds, then refresh in cold water. Peel away the skins and chop. Add the sliced zucchini, chickpeas and tomatoes to the other vegetables and cook for another 10 minutes. Stir in the cilantro and season with salt and pepper. Keep hot.

 To cook the couscous, bring 2 cups water to a boil in a large saucepan. Add the remaining oil and the salt. Remove from the heat and add the couscous, stirring. Let swell for 2 minutes, then add the butter and heat through gently, stirring to separate the grains.

5 Turn the couscous out onto a warm serving dish and spoon the vegetables on top, pouring any liquid over. Garnish and serve.

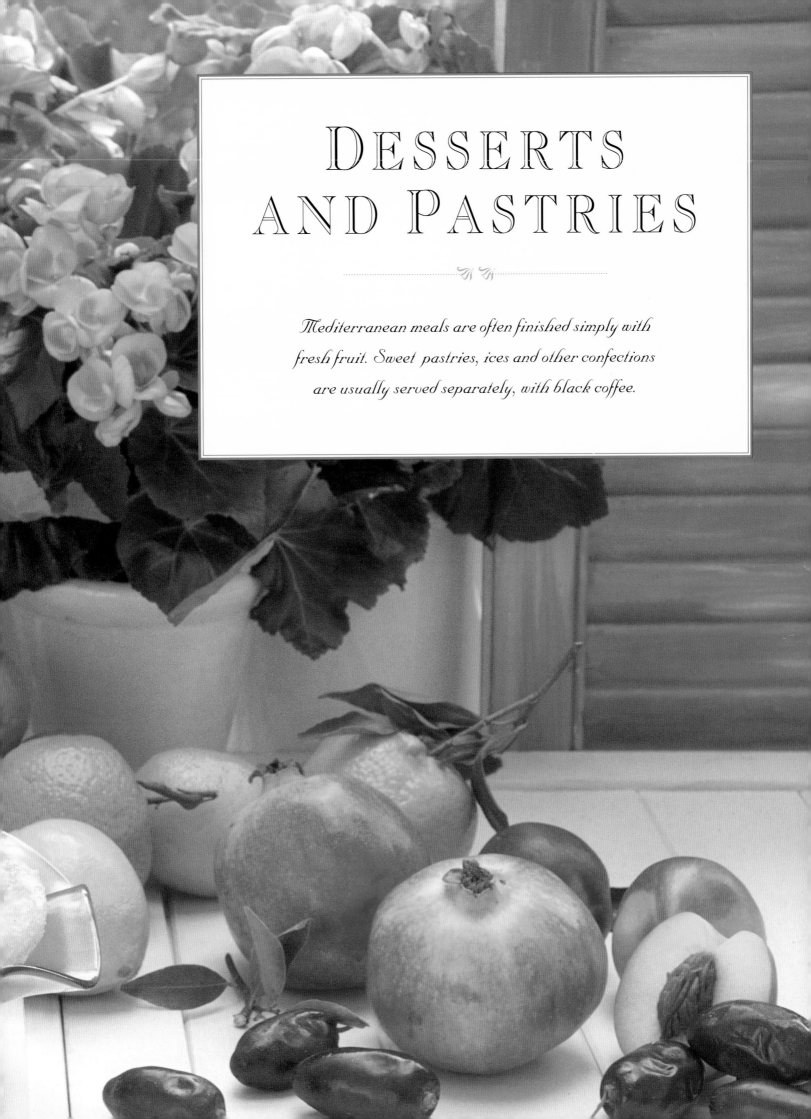

DESSERTS AND PASTRIES

Mediterranean meals are often finished simply with fresh fruit. Sweet pastries, ices and other confections are usually served separately, with black coffee.

A peep in the glass display cabinets of any pâtisserie, confectioner or coffeehouse just about anywhere around the Mediterranean will reveal an absolute feast of sweet treats. From highly decorated cakes and tortes, lavishly finished with sugared decorations, to the painstakingly stuffed and glazed or candied fruits, all Mediterranean sweets offer an abundance of fabulous flavors. Many desserts, pastries and confections involve complex cooking techniques and need specialized ingredients, and they are perhaps best left to the skills of professional pastry chefs. These include some of the lavish, multi-flavored ice cream gâteaux of Italy and a number of the specialized pastries of the Arab world.

On a domestic level, most Mediterranean desserts take full advantage of the glorious abundance of fresh fruits. For a special occasion, a colorful selection of seasonal fruits such as figs, plums, apricots, peaches, melons and cherries makes a stunning finale. These can be arranged on a platter lined with grape or fig leaves with some of the fruits cut open decoratively, and the whole platter scattered with crushed ice. On a simpler scale, pomegranate seeds or sweet juicy oranges can be arranged in bowls, sprinkled with sugar and rose water or orange-

BELOW: Orange groves abound in this fertile valley near Jaén in Spain.

ABOVE: Pyramids of gorgeous fruit await the shopper at the covered market in Florence.

ABOVE: Plump, rosy and ready for picking, peaches make a perfect dessert, alone or with a delicious amaretto stuffing.

flower water and served iced. Fresh fruits can also be lightly poached in sugar- or honey-sweetened syrups, sometimes with the addition of mild spices. They'll store well for several days as the syrup becomes impregnated with the flavors of the fruit and spices. Pears, quinces, apricots and figs are typical examples. Other refreshing desserts are the smooth sorbets of France and the granitas of Italy, or the broiled or baked fruits that are so full of flavor. Sometimes these are sugared or topped with a scoop of mascarpone or ricotta and laced with a little liqueur. A selection of dried fruits, available in abundance and of good quality, makes an ideal end to a meal when served with dessert wine or liqueurs.

In Turkey, Greece, Lebanon and Egypt, small sweet pastries and confections are enjoyed as a between-meal snack with good strong coffee. These include the rich pastries, doughnuts, and semolina and nut cakes, drenched in spiced syrup and featuring flavors like honey, almonds, pistachios, sesame, pine nuts, rose water and orange-flower water. Served in small pieces, they make a wonderful contrast to the bitterness of the coffee. The Semolina and Nut Halva is a light version of a syrupy steeped cake which that is perfect with coffee or as a dessert with cream.

Other prominent Mediterranean desserts are the sweet milk-based puddings of both the east and the west. In North Africa and the Middle East these are made with ground or short-grain rice and spiced with cinnamon, cloves, anise or fennel. They are usually served cold, sometimes drizzled with a honey-and-orange-flavored syrup. One of Spain's classic desserts is the elegant Crema Catalana, a sweet, creamy custard that is absolutely delicious either on its own or accompanied by fresh or sweetened fruits.

FRESH FIGS WITH HONEY AND WINE

Any variety of figs can be used in this recipe, their ripeness determining the cooking time. Choose ones that are plump and firm, and use them quickly because they don't keep well.

2 cups dry white wine
⅓ cup honey
¼ cup sugar
1 small orange
8 whole cloves
1 pound fresh figs
1 cinnamon stick
mint sprigs or bay leaves, to decorate

FOR THE CREAM
1¼ cups heavy cream
1 vanilla bean
1 teaspoon sugar

SERVES 6

1 Put the wine, honey and sugar in a heavy saucepan and heat gently until the sugar dissolves.

2 Stud the orange with the cloves and add to the syrup with the figs and cinnamon. Cover and simmer very gently for 5–10 minutes, until the figs are softened. Transfer to a serving dish and let cool.

3 Put ⅔ cup of the cream in a small saucepan with the vanilla bean. Bring almost to a boil, then let cool and infuse for 30 minutes. Remove the vanilla bean and mix with the remaining cream and sugar in a bowl. Whip lightly. Transfer to a serving dish. Decorate the figs, then serve with the cream.

CHURROS

These Spanish doughnuts are commercially deep-fried in huge coils and broken off into smaller pieces for selling. Serve this homemade version freshly cooked with hot chocolate or strong coffee.

1¾ cups all-purpose flour
¼ teaspoon salt
2 tablespoons sugar
¼ cup olive or sunflower oil
1 egg, beaten
sugar and ground cinnamon
for dusting
oil for deep-frying

MAKES 12–15

1 Sift the flour, salt and sugar onto a plate or piece of paper. Heat 1 cup of water in a saucepan with the oil until it boils.

2 Pour in the flour mixture and beat with a wooden spoon until the mixture forms a stiff paste. Let cool for 2 minutes.

3 Gradually beat in the egg until smooth. Oil a large baking sheet. Sprinkle plenty of sugar onto a plate and stir in a little cinnamon.

4 Put the dough in a large pastry bag fitted with a ½-inch plain piping nozzle. Pipe little coils or S shapes onto the baking sheet.

5 Heat 2 inches of oil in a large pan to 336°F or until a little dough sizzles on the surface.

6 Using an oiled metal spatula, lower several of the piped shapes into the oil and cook for about 2 minutes, until light golden.

7 Drain on paper towels, then coat with the sugar and cinnamon mixture. Cook the remaining churros in the same way and serve immediately.

WALNUT AND RICOTTA CAKE

Soft, tangy ricotta cheese is widely used in Italian desserts. Here, it is included along with walnuts and orange to flavor a sponge cake. Don't worry if it sinks slightly after baking—this gives it an authentic appearance.

1 cup walnut pieces
10 tablespoons unsalted butter, softened
⅔ cup sugar
5 eggs, separated
finely grated zest of 1 orange
⅔ cup ricotta cheese
6 tablespoons all-purpose flour

TO FINISH
¼ cup apricot jam
2 tablespoons brandy
2 ounces unsweetened or semisweet chocolate, coarsely grated

MAKES 10 SLICES

1 Preheat the oven to 375°F. Grease and line the bottom of a deep 9-inch round, removable-bottomed cake pan. Coarsely chop and lightly toast the walnuts.

2 Cream together the butter and ½ cup of the sugar until light and fluffy. Add the egg yolks, orange zest, ricotta cheese, flour and walnuts and combine.

3 Beat the egg whites in a large bowl until stiff. Gradually beat in the remaining sugar. Using a large metal spoon, fold a quarter of the beaten whites into the ricotta mixture. Carefully fold in the rest of the beaten whites.

4 Turn the mixture out into the prepared pan and level the surface. Bake for about 30 minutes, until risen and firm. Let the cake cool in the pan.

5 Transfer the cake to a serving plate. Heat the apricot jam in a small saucepan with 1 tablespoon water. Strain and stir in the brandy. Use to coat the top and sides of the cake. Scatter grated chocolate generously over the cake.

VARIATION
Use toasted and chopped almonds in place of the walnuts.

BISCOTTI

These Italian cookies are baked, sliced to reveal a feast of mixed nuts and then baked again until crisp and golden. Traditionally they're served dipped in vin santo, a sweet dessert wine—perfect for rounding off a Mediterranean meal.

4 tablespoons unsalted butter,
softened
½ cup sugar
1½ cups self-rising flour
¼ teaspoon salt
2 teaspoons baking powder
1 teaspoon ground coriander
finely grated zest of 1 lemon
½ cup polenta
1 egg, lightly beaten
2 teaspoons brandy or orange-
flavored liqueur
½ cup unblanched almonds
½ cup pistachios

MAKES 24

1 Preheat the oven to 325°F. Lightly grease a baking sheet. Cream together the butter and sugar in a bowl.

2 Sift all the flour, salt, baking powder and coriander into the bowl. Add the lemon zest, polenta, egg and brandy or liqueur and combine to make a soft dough.

3 Stir in the nuts until evenly combined. Halve the mixture. Shape each half into a flat sausage about 9 inches long and 2½ inches wide. Bake for about 30 minutes, until risen and just firm. Remove from oven.

4 When cool, cut each sausage diagonally into 12 thin slices. Return to the baking sheet and cook for another 10 minutes, until crisp.

5 Transfer to a wire rack to cool completely. Store in an airtight jar for up to 1 week.

COOK'S TIP
Use a sharp, serrated knife to slice the cooled cookies, otherwise they will crumble.

SEMOLINA AND NUT HALVA

Semolina is a popular ingredient in many desserts and pastries in the eastern Mediterranean. Here it provides a spongy base for soaking up a deliciously fragrant, spicy syrup.

1 Preheat the oven to 425°F. Grease and line the bottom of a deep 9-inch square cake pan.

2 Lightly cream the butter in a bowl. Add the sugar, orange zest and juice, eggs, semolina, baking powder and hazelnuts and beat the ingredients together until smooth.

5 Bring to a boil and boil rapidly, without stirring, for 5 minutes. Measure half the boiling syrup and add the lemon juice and orange-flower water to it. Pour over the halva. Reserve the remainder of the syrup in the pan.

6 Leave the halva in the pan until the syrup is absorbed, then turn it out onto a plate and cut diagonally into diamond-shaped portions. Sprinkle with the nuts.

FOR THE HALVA
8 tablespoons (1 stick) unsalted butter, softened
½ cup sugar
finely grated zest of 1 orange, plus 2 tablespoons juice
3 eggs
1 cup semolina
2 teaspoons baking powder
1 cup ground hazelnuts

TO FINISH
1½ cups sugar
2 cinnamon sticks, halved
juice of 1 lemon
¼ cup orange-flower water
½ cup unblanched hazelnuts, toasted and chopped
½ cup blanched almonds, toasted and chopped
shredded zest of 1 orange
SERVES 10

3 Put into the prepared pan and level the surface. Bake for 20–25 minutes, until just firm and golden. Let cool in the pan.

4 To make the syrup, put the sugar in a small, heavy saucepan with 2¼ cups water and the half cinnamon sticks. Heat gently, stirring, until the sugar has dissolved completely.

7 Boil the remaining syrup until slightly thickened, then pour it on the halva. Sprinkle the shredded orange zest on the cake and serve with lightly whipped cream.

COOK'S TIP
Be sure to use a deep, solid cake pan rather than one with a removable bottom; otherwise, the syrup might seep out.

CREMA CATALANA

*This delicious Spanish dessert is a cross between a crème caramel and a crème brûlée. It is not as rich
as crème brûlée, but has a similar caramelized sugar topping.*

*2 cups milk
pared zest of ½ lemon
1 cinnamon stick
4 egg yolks
7 tablespoons sugar
1½ tablespoons cornstarch
ground nutmeg*

SERVES 4

1 Put the milk in a pan with the lemon zest and cinnamon stick. Bring to a boil, then simmer for 10 minutes. Remove the lemon zest and cinnamon. Place the egg yolks and 3 tablespoons of the sugar in a bowl and whisk until pale yellow. Add the cornstarch and mix well.

2 Stir in a few tablespoons of the hot milk, then add this mixture to the remaining milk. Return to the heat and cook gently, stirring, for about 5 minutes, until thickened and smooth. Do not let it boil. There should be no cornstarch taste.

3 Pour into 4 shallow ovenproof dishes, about 5 inches in diameter. Let cool, then chill for a few hours or overnight if possible, until firm. Before serving, sprinkle each custard with a tablespoon of sugar and a little of the ground nutmeg. Preheat the broiler to high.

4 Place the custards under the broiler, on the highest shelf, and cook until the sugar caramelizes. This will only take a few seconds. Let cool for a few minutes before serving. (The caramel will only stay hard for about 30 minutes.)

MOROCCAN RICE PUDDING

A simple and delicious alternative to a traditional rice pudding. The rice is cooked in almond-flavored milk and delicately flavored with cinnamon and orange-flower water.

¼ cup blanched almonds, chopped

2¼ cups short-grain rice

¼ cup confectioners' sugar

3-inch cinnamon stick

4 tablespoons butter

pinch of salt

¼ teaspoon almond extract

¾ cup milk

¾ cup sweetened condensed milk

2 tablespoons orange-flower water

toasted sliced almonds and ground cinnamon, to decorate

SERVES 6

1   Put the chopped almonds in a food processor or blender with ¼ cup of very hot water. Process, then strain into a bowl. Return the almonds to the food processor or blender, add another ¼ cup very hot water, and process again. Strain into a saucepan.

2   Add 1¼ cups of water to the almond "milk" and bring to a boil. Combine the other milks. Add the rice, sugar, cinnamon and half the butter, the salt, the almond extract, and half the mixed milks.

3   Bring to a boil, then simmer, covered, for about 30 minutes, adding more milk if necessary. Continue to cook the rice, stirring and adding the remaining milk, until it becomes thick and creamy. Stir in the orange-flower water, then taste the rice pudding for sweetness, adding extra sugar, if necessary.

4   Pour the rice pudding into a serving bowl and sprinkle with the sliced almonds. Dot with the remaining butter and dust with ground cinnamon. Serve hot.

TURKISH DELIGHT ICE CREAM

Not strictly a traditional Middle Eastern recipe, but a delicious way of using Turkish delight.
Serve scattered with rose petals, if you can find them.

4 egg yolks
½ cup sugar
1¼ cups milk
1¼ cups heavy cream
1 tablespoon rose water
6 ounces rose-flavored Turkish
delight, chopped

SERVES 6

1 Beat the egg yolks and sugar until light. In a pan, bring the milk to a boil. Add to the egg and sugar, stirring, then return to the pan.

2 Continue stirring over low heat until the mixture coats the back of a spoon. Do not boil, or it will curdle. Let cool, then stir in the cream and rose water.

3 Put the Turkish delight in a pan with 2–3 tablespoons water. Heat gently, until almost completely melted, with just a few small lumps. Remove from the heat and stir into the cooled custard mixture.

4 Let the mixture cool completely, then pour into a shallow freezer container. Freeze for 3 hours, until just frozen all over. Spoon the mixture into a bowl.

5 Using a whisk, beat the mixture well, return it to the freezer container and freeze for 2 hours more. Repeat the beating process, then return to the freezer for about 3 hours or until firm. Remove the ice cream from the freezer 20–25 minutes before serving. Serve with thin almond cookies or meringues.

ICED ORANGES

These little sherbets served in the fruit shell were originally sold in the beach cafés in the south of France.
They are pretty and easy to eat—a good picnic treat to store in the cooler.

⅔ cup sugar
juice of 1 lemon
14 medium oranges
8 fresh bay leaves, to decorate

SERVES 8

1 Put the sugar in a heavy pan. Add half the lemon juice and ½ cup water. Cook over low heat until the sugar has dissolved completely. Bring to a boil and boil for 2–3 minutes, until the syrup is clear. Let cool.

2 Slice the tops off eight of the oranges to make "hats." Scoop out the flesh of the oranges and reserve. Put the empty orange shells and "hats" on a tray and place in the freezer until needed.

3 Grate the zest of the remaining oranges and add to the syrup. Squeeze the juice from the oranges and from the reserved flesh. There should be 3 cups. Squeeze another orange or add bought orange juice, if necessary.

4 Stir the orange juice and remaining lemon juice, with 6 tablespoons water, into the syrup. Taste, adding more lemon juice or sugar, as desired. Pour the mixture into a shallow freezer container and freeze for 3 hours.

5 Transfer the mixture into a bowl and whisk to break down the ice crystals. Freeze for 4 more hours, until firm but not solid.

6 Pack the mixture into the orange shells, piling it up, and set the "hats" on top. Freeze until ready to serve. Just before serving, push a skewer into the tops of the "hats" and push a bay leaf into each one.

COOK'S TIP
Use crumpled paper towels to keep the shells upright.

STUFFED PEACHES WITH MASCARPONE CREAM

Mascarpone is a thick, velvety Italian cream cheese made from cow's milk. It is often used in desserts or eaten with fresh fruit.

4 large peaches, halved and pitted
1½ ounces amaretti cookies, crumbled
2 tablespoons ground almonds
3 tablespoons sugar
1 tablespoon cocoa powder
⅔ cup sweet wine
2 tablespoons butter

FOR THE MASCARPONE CREAM
2 tablespoons sugar
3 egg yolks
1 tablespoon dessert wine
1 cup mascarpone cheese
⅔ cup heavy cream

SERVES 4

1 Preheat the oven to 400°F. Using a teaspoon, scoop some of the flesh from the cavities in the peaches, to make a reasonable space for stuffing. Chop the scooped-out peach flesh.

2 Combine the amaretti, ground almonds, sugar, cocoa and peach flesh. Add enough wine to make the mixture into a thick paste.

3 Place the peaches in a buttered ovenproof dish and fill them with the stuffing. Dot with the butter, then pour the remaining wine into the dish. Bake for 35 minutes.

4 To make the mascarpone cream, beat the sugar and egg yolks until thick and pale. Stir in the wine, then fold in the mascarpone. Whip the heavy cream to soft peaks and fold into the mixture. Remove the peaches from the oven and let them cool. Serve at room temperature, with the mascarpone cream.

CHERRY CLAFOUTI

When fresh cherries are in season this makes a deliciously simple dessert for any occasion. Serve warm with a little cream.

1½ pounds fresh cherries
½ cup all-purpose flour
pinch of salt
4 eggs, plus 2 egg yolks
½ cup sugar
2½ cups milk
4 tablespoons butter, melted
sugar for dusting

SERVES 6

1 Preheat the oven to 375°F. Lightly butter the bottom and sides of a shallow ovenproof dish. Pit the cherries and place in the dish.

2 Sift the flour and salt into a bowl. Add the eggs, egg yolks, sugar and a little of the milk and whisk to a smooth batter.

3 Gradually whisk in the rest of the milk and the rest of the butter, then strain the batter over the cherries. Bake for 40–50 minutes, until golden and just set. Serve warm, dusted with sugar, if desired.

VARIATION
Use two 15-ounce cans pitted black cherries, thoroughly drained, if fresh cherries are not available. For a special dessert, add 3 tablespoons kirsch to the batter.

COFFEE GRANITA

Granitas are like semi-frozen sherbets, but consist of larger particles of ice. Served in Italian cafés,
they are very refreshing, particularly in the summer. Some are made with fruit, but the coffee version is
perhaps the most popular and is often served with a spoonful of whipped cream on top.

1½ cups hot strong
espresso coffee
2 tablespoons granulated sugar
1 cup heavy cream
2 teaspoons superfine sugar

SERVES 6–8

1 Stir the sugar into the hot coffee until dissolved. Let cool, then chill. Pour into a shallow plastic or metal freezer container, cover and freeze for about 1 hour.

2 The coffee should have formed a frozen crust around the rim of the container. Scrape this off with a spoon and mix with the rest of the coffee. Repeat this process every 30 minutes, using the spoon to break up the clumps of ice.

3 After about 2½ hours, the granita should be ready. It will have the appearance of small, fairly uniform ice crystals. Whip the cream with the superfine sugar until stiff. Serve the granita in tall glasses, each topped with a spoonful of cream.

DATE AND ALMOND TART

Fresh dates make an unusual but delicious filling for a tart. The influences here are French and Middle Eastern—a true Mediterranean fusion!

FOR THE PASTRY
1½ cups all-purpose flour
6 tablespoons butter
1 egg

FOR THE FILLING
scant 8 tablespoons (1 stick) butter
7 tablespoons sugar
1 egg, beaten
scant 1 cup ground almonds
2 tablespoons flour
2 tablespoons orange-flower water
12–13 fresh dates, halved
and pitted
¼ cup apricot jam

SERVES 6

1 Preheat the oven to 400°F. Place a baking sheet in the oven. Sift the flour into a bowl, add the butter and work with your fingertips until the mixture resembles fine bread crumbs. Add the egg and a tablespoon of cold water, then work to a smooth dough.

4 Spread the mixture evenly over the bottom of the pastry shell. Arrange the dates, cut side down, on the almond mixture. Bake on the hot baking sheet for 10–15 minutes, then reduce the heat to 350°F. Bake for another 15–20 minutes, until light golden and set.

2 Roll out the pastry on a lightly floured surface and use to line an 8-inch tart pan. Prick the bottom with a fork, then chill until needed.

5 Transfer the tart to a rack to cool. Gently heat the apricot jam, then strain. Add the remaining orange-flower water.

3 To make the filling, cream the butter and sugar until light, then beat in the egg. Stir in the ground almonds, flour and 1 tablespoon of the orange-flower water, mixing well.

6 Brush the tart with the jam and serve at room temperature.

LEMON TART

This is one of the classic French desserts, and it is hard to beat—a rich lemon curd is encased in flaky pastry. Crème fraîche is an optional accompaniment.

3   Roll the pastry out on a floured surface and use to line a 9-inch tart pan. Line with foil or waxed paper and fill with dried beans or rice, or baking beans if you have them. Bake for 10 minutes.

FOR THE PASTRY
2 cups all-purpose flour
8 tablespoons (1 stick) butter
2 tablespoons confectioners' sugar
1 egg
1 teaspoon vanilla extract

FOR THE FILLING
6 eggs, beaten
1½ cups sugar
8 tablespoons (1 stick) unsalted butter
grated zest and juice of 4 lemons
confectioners' sugar, for dusting

SERVES 6

1   Preheat the oven to 400°F. Sift the flour into a bowl, add the butter and work with your fingertips until the mixture resembles fine bread crumbs. Stir in the 2 tablespoons of confectioners' sugar.

4   To make the filling, put the eggs, sugar and butter into a pan and stir over low heat until the sugar has dissolved completely. Add the lemon zest and juice and continue cooking, stirring constantly, until the lemon curd has thickened slightly.

2   Add the egg, vanilla extract and a scant tablespoon of cold water, then work to a dough.

5   Pour the mixture into the pastry shell. Bake for 20 minutes, until just set. Transfer the tart to a wire rack to cool. Dust with confectioners' sugar just before serving.

HONEY AND PINE NUT TART

Wonderful tarts of all descriptions are to be found throughout France. This recipe recalls the flavors of the south.

FOR THE PASTRY
2 cups all-purpose flour
8 tablespoons (1 stick) butter
2 tablespoons confectioners' sugar
1 egg

FOR THE FILLING
¾ pound (3 sticks) unsalted butter, diced
½ cup granulated sugar
3 eggs, beaten
⅔ cup sunflower or other flower honey
grated zest and juice of 1 lemon
2⅔ cups pine nuts
pinch of salt
confectioners' sugar for dusting

SERVES 6

1 Preheat the oven to 350°F. Sift the flour into a bowl, add the butter and work with your fingertips until the mixture resembles fine bread crumbs. Stir in the confectioners' sugar. Add the egg and 1 tablespoon of water and work to a firm dough that leaves the bowl clean.

3 Cream together the butter and sugar until light. Beat in the eggs one by one. Gently heat the honey in a small saucepan until runny, then add to the butter mixture with the lemon zest and juice. Stir in the pine nuts and salt, then pour the filling into the pastry shell.

2 Roll out the pastry on a floured surface and use to line a 9-inch tart pan. Prick the bottom with a fork and chill for 10 minutes. Line with foil or waxed paper and fill with dried beans or rice, or baking beans if you have them. Bake the pastry shell for 10 minutes.

4 Bake for about 45 minutes, until the filling is lightly browned and set. Let cool slightly in the pan, then dust generously with confectioners' sugar. Serve warm or at room temperature, with sour cream or vanilla ice cream.

GLAZED PRUNE TART

Generously glazed, creamy custard tarts are a pâtisserie favorite all over France. Plump prunes, heavily laced with brandy or kirsch, add a wonderful taste and texture to this deliciously sweet and creamy filling.

1 cup pitted prunes
¼ cup brandy or kirsch

FOR THE SWEET PASTRY
1½ cups all-purpose flour
pinch of salt
8 tablespoons (1 stick) unsalted butter
2 tablespoons sugar
2 egg yolks

FOR THE FILLING
⅔ cup heavy cream
⅔ cup milk
1 vanilla bean
3 eggs
¼ cup sugar

TO FINISH
¼ cup apricot jam
1 tablespoon brandy or kirsch
confectioners' sugar for dusting

SERVES 8

1 Put the prunes in a bowl with the brandy or kirsch and let sit for about 4 hours, until most of the liqueur has been absorbed.

2 To make the pastry, sift the flour and salt into a bowl. Add the butter, cut into small pieces, and rub in with the fingertips. Stir in the sugar and egg yolks and mix to a dough using a round-bladed knife.

3 Turn the dough out onto a lightly floured surface and knead to a smooth ball. Wrap tightly and chill for 30 minutes.

4 Preheat the oven to 400°F. Roll out the pastry on a lightly floured surface and use to line a 10-inch springform tart pan.

5 Line with waxed paper and fill with dried beans or rice, or baking beans if you have them. Bake for 15 minutes. Remove the beans and paper and bake for another 5 minutes.

6 Arrange the prunes, evenly spaced, in the pastry shell, reserving any liqueur left in the bowl.

7 For the filling, put the cream and milk in a saucepan with the vanilla bean and bring to a boil. Turn off the heat and let the mixture infuse for 15 minutes.

8 Whisk together the eggs and sugar in a bowl. Remove the vanilla bean from the cream and return the cream to a boil. Pour on the eggs and sugar, whisking to make a smooth custard.

9 Cool slightly, then pour the custard over the prunes. Bake the tart for about 25 minutes, until the filling is lightly set and turning golden around the edges.

10 Strain the apricot jam into a small pan. Add the liqueur and heat through gently. Use to glaze the tart. Serve warm or cold, dusted with confectioners' sugar.

COOK'S TIP
The vanilla bean can be washed and dried, ready for use another time. Alternatively, use 1 teaspoon vanilla or almond extract.

INDEX

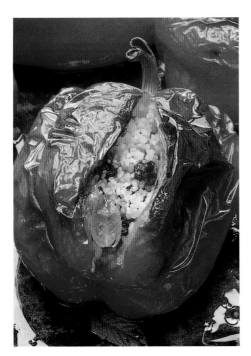

INDEX

Photographs: With the exceptions noted below, all photographs by Michelle Garrett:
Patrick McLeavey: p.10 (top right): The Image Bank: p.1, p.9 (bottom left), p.20 (top left),
p.108 (left), p.198, p.227 (right); The Anthony Blake Photo Library: p.9 (top right), p.138,
p.139, p.171 (top right), p.171 (bottom left), p.227 (left); Robert Estall: p.2, p.6–7, p.8;
Michael Busselle: p.87, p.170, p.226